The Door of the Beloved: Poems of Hafiz

Translated by Justin McCarthy

Also Available from Bardic Press

New Nightingale, New Rose:
Poems From the Divan of Hafiz
translated by Richard Le Gallienne

The Quatrains of Omar Khayyam:
Three Translations of the Rubaiyat
translated by Edward Fitzgerald, Justin McCarthy
and Richard Le gallienne

Christ in Islam
James Robson

The Four Branches of the Mabinogi:
Celtic Myth and Medieval Reality
Will Parker

Boyhood With Gurdjieff; Gurdjieff Remembered;
Balanced Man
Fritz Peters

Don't Forget: P.D. Ouspensky's Life of Self-remembering
Bob Hunter

Visit our website at www.bardic-press.com
email us at info@bardic-press.com

The Door of the Beloved: Poems of Hafiz

Translated by Justin McCarthy

Bardic Press
California, 2006

Published by Bardic Press
PO Box 761
Oregon House
CA 95962
USA
http://www.Bardic-Press.com
info@bardic-press.com

ISBN 0-9745667-9-9

Foreword

Justin Huntley McCarthy (1830-1912) was a Parnellite Irish MP at the end of the nineteenth century. His writing career began at the age of 16, when he worked as a reporter for a local newspaper. As well as his translation of Hafiz he made a prose translation of Omar Khayyám, also published by Bardic Press in the volume *The Quatrains of Omar Khayyám: Three Translations of the Rubaiyat.* McCarthy learned Persian specifically to translate Khayyám, and produced an extensive translation in a literal and elegant prose. His translation of Khayyám contains a total of 566 quatrains, making it the most extensive English translation of Khayyám.

McCarthy's translation of Hafiz is in elegant and literal prose, but he had a tendency towards language that even at the end of the nineteenth century was archaic, and occasionally even eccentric. For this edition his archaicisms have been modernised, but his rhythm and meaning have been preserved. Hafiz is not a poet to be captured in a single translation. McCarthy's elegant prose gives us a direct Hafiz, full of clear imagery and personal poetry.

Hafiz was born around 1320AD in Shiraz, Persia. He was a contemporary of other fourteenth century notables such as Chaucer and Petrarch and, in the Islamic world, of the infamous conqueror Tamerlane, and of the poets Ibn-I-Yamin and Salman-I-Sawaji. Hafiz is a title for someone who has memorised the entire Koran: the poet's given name was Shams-ud-din Mohammed. Hafiz lived in a time of political commotion, of coups and upheavals, though Shiraz escaped the worst results of the invasions of the Mongols and the Tartars. His father died when he was relatively young and he had two older brothers; between the three of them they supported the family. Hafiz was bright, yet he had to work first for a draper and then at a bakery to help support the family. He is said to have written his first poem by completing a poem begun by his untalented uncle.

While there is little in the way of hard historical fact, a number of anecdotes are told of Hafiz, many of them with a legendary or symbolic quality. The most famous of them is as follows. When he was twenty-one, and working as a baker, Hafiz was delivering bread in a prosperous district of Shiraz. While doing his deliveries, he saw a beautiful woman and, of course, fell hopelessly in love with her. He was not a physically attractive man, nor, as a baker's boy, wealthy, and had little chance of successfully wooing her. Hafiz began to write poems about her, and the poems circulated and became popular in Shiraz. He was still as hopelessly in love with her as before but, even though she knew of his poetry, the love was unrequited.

There are a number of different versions of this story. According to the most developed version, Hafiz knew of a legend that told that anyone who could spend forty nights without sleep at the tomb of Baba Kuhi, a saint who died centuries earlier, would be granted his heart's desire. (A similar legend in Wales tells that whoever spends a night alone in certain places will the next morning be found dead, mad or will become a poet; the forty nights also reminds us of Jesus's forty days and nights in the wilderness, and of Moses's forty years in the desert.) Hafiz decided to keep this forty night sleepless vigil, even though, as a man who lived in the world, he had to work for the bakery during the day. He went to the tomb night after night, and by the end of the forty nights he was almost walking in his sleep. On the very last night, Shakh-I-Nabat, "the branch of sugarcane", the woman with whom Hafiz had fallen in love and for whom he was keeping this vigil, came to him as he was on his way to the saint's tomb, and declared her love for him, impressed as she was by his poems written of her, and his persistence. But Hafiz could only think of completing his vigil and staggered towards the tomb to spend his last sleepless night there.

At dawn the next day, the angel Gabriel appeared and asked Hafiz what his heart's desire was. Instead of telling Gabriel that he wished his beloved Shakh-I-Nabat, he declared that, since God's angel, Gabriel, was so beautiful, then God must be even more beautiful. Hafiz exclaimed, "I wish God." Gabriel then directed Hafiz to a small grocery store where he would find a man named Attar, who became his teacher. Attar taught Hafiz for the next forty years. (Incidentally, this is not the same Attar as the famous, and earlier, author of the Conference of the Birds.)

Hafiz married and had at least one son, but it is not clear whether he married Shakh-I-Nabat or another woman. His poems became widely known, and he taught the Koran and became a court poet to Abou Ishak, the governor of Shiraz. Abou Ishak (who appears in poem 174) loved wine, poetry and pleasure so much that he neglected government and soon lost his kingdom to Mubariz Muzaffar. The capture of Shiraz by Mubariz Muzaffar resulted in Hafiz losing both of his positions. Muzaffar was a Sunni puritan who ordered the wine taverns to be closed: "It is a wonderful and wicked thing They at this season should the tavern close; Drink shall we none the less—under the rose; The Water of Life runs from this little spring." Yet another coup followed and Hafiz regained his position again when Muzaffar's son, Shah Shuja, overthrew his father. Shah Shuja reopened the taverns. This was the time when Hafiz was most prolific in his writing, but after a few years, he fell out of favour with his new master, and went in exile to Isfahan. He was allowed to return four years later.

Hafiz's wife and son both died within his lifetime, his .son seemingly in childhood. He wife is thought to be commemorated in poems 227 and 598, his son in poem 606. Hafiz was Attar's pupil all this time, even though he was separated from him by exile. According to the story, when he was sixty years old Hafiz became tired of his forty year discipleship, and tired of waiting for union with God. In a move that echoes his forty night vigil, he drew a circle on the ground and stayed within it for forty days. At the end of this period, Gabriel appeared again to him, and asked him what he wished. By this time, Hafiz could only say that he wished to serve his teacher. He then returned to Attar's house, and his teacher greeted him with a cup of old wine. On drinking it Hafiz finally attained union with God.

In one of the great crossings of history (or legend), Hafiz met Tamerlane, the bloody conqueror celebrated in Marlowe's Tamburlaine plays. It is a moment that reminds us of Alexander the Great sparing the house in Thebes where Pindar had lived, or of Goethe's meeting with Napoleon. In one of his most famous poems, Hafiz had written to his beloved, in Le Gallienne's translation, "I'll give to you Bokhara—yes! and Samarkand. Indeed, I'd give them for the mole upon your cheek."Tamerlane came from Samarkand and had conquered both cities. He asked Hafiz why he would give up these great cities for the mole on the cheek of a woman from Shiraz—wasn't this an insult to the conqueror? Hafiz, who was poor and had been unable to pay the tax demanded by Tamerlane's forces, replied, "It is because of such generosity that I find myself in such poverty!"

Hafiz died in 1389, and his tomb is in the garden of Musalla, through which the stream Rukbnabad flows. Both are celebrated in his poetry, and both are now famous because of him.

Andrew Phillip Smith

I

A city it is, fair with gracious forms; a picture on every side! Friends, my friends, it is the salutation of love, if you desire to traffic.

The eye of Heaven will never gaze on fresher youth than this: a fairer quarry has never yet been delivered into the hands of the hunter!

Who has ever beheld earthly forms, so like spirit? May no dust of mortality defile their raiment.

Wherefore do you cast out from your presence one so crushed as I am? Great was my hope of a kiss or an embrace.

The wine is of good vintage, drink quickly; using the propitious hour! Another year, who can count on another springtime?

The guests are gathered in the garden, comrades of the tulip and the rose; each filling a cup to the memory of the face of his loved one.

How shall I disentangle this knot? how solve this mystery?—hard, very hard it is! —a problem troublesome, very troublesome.

Each thread of the hair of Hafiz is woven in the web of a laughing girl's tresses; it is very perilous to abide in a city like this!

II

Again the wine has stolen from me my self-possession; again the wine has conquered me by its caresses.

A thousand blessings on the red wine, which has driven from my face its sallow colour!

Benedictions on the hand which gathered the grape—may the foot which pressed it never fail!

Love was written on my forehead by the finger of Fate: the Fate which is once written it is impossible to cancel!

Babble not about wisdom, for in the day of death Aristotle must yield up his soul like the miserable beggar.

Go, pious man, and blame me not, for what God has made is no small matter.

Waste not your life in such a way in this world, that when you are dead men shall say nothing but—"Dead!"

Intoxicated with "Unity" from the cup of "Eternity" will all be who drink pure wine like Hafiz.

III

Although I am old, and weak, and weary, whenever I remember your face I become young once more.

Thanks be to God, that whenever I have asked anything righteously of God, my prayer has prospered.

On the Eternal road of Destiny I have mounted the throne of Fortune, as was the wish of my friends, holding a cup of wine.

O young rosebush, enjoy, while you may, the fruit of pleasure; for beneath your shelter I became the nightingale of the garden of the world!

Once no voice or letter had given word of me to the world; it was in the school of sorrow for you that I became thus subtle.

From the moment that the enchantment of your eye fell upon me, I was safe from all enchantment to the end of time.

That day the door of reality was thrown open to my heart, when I became one of those who dwelt in your court.

It was decreed to be my fate to become a haunter of the tavern; into this path I entered, and such did I become!

It was not years and months that aged me—it was my unfaithful friend! She it was who, like passing life, made me an old man.

Last night the Master sent me a joyful message: "Return, Hafiz: I will be the surety that your sin shall be pardoned."

IV

At early dawn, after a night of wine, I seized the lute, the cup, and the flagon. I gave to Wisdom provision for its journey, and urged it on its way to the City of Intoxication.

The seller of wine beheld me with caressing glances, so that I felt free from the deceit of Time.

Then from the arch-eyebrowed cupbearer I heard, "O you who are a target for the arrow of reproach,

"Never will you, like a girdle, gain profit from that waist, so long as you see therein nothing but yourself."

Go, spread your snare before some other bird; the eagle builds its nest in an exalted place!

The companion, the minstrel, the cupbearer—are all only phantoms of clay and water; all nothing, save illusion.

Bring me a bowl of wine, that I may steer in safety out of this sea without shore!

Who gains a gracious reward from the fair one who is for ever playing at love with herself!

O Hafiz, our life is a riddle; the attempt to read it a delusion and a vain tale!

V

A thousand thanks, that I have once more gazed on you as I wished: that with loyalty and purity you are again become the partner of my soul!

Wayfarers must sometimes tread the Path of Calamity: the companion of the Path must not consider the ascent and the descent.

The grief of a hidden passion is better than the search for the watcher; for to the breasts of the malicious are not to be confided such secrets.

Rejoice that the assembly is illuminated by the presence of the loved one: if you are badly treated, imitate the taper; be wasted, but still burn.

With a half kiss purchase a blessing from one who has a heart; for this will save you body and soul from the machinations of your enemy.

The sadness that has shadowed my countenance from the pain you have caused me, would take me, beloved, a long year to relate.

The song of love has made known in Iraq and Hijaz the sweet melody of the ghazels of Hafiz of Shiraz.

VI

A brace of good comrades, a flagon of wine, leisure, and a book, and a corner of the garden.

I would not barter this state either for this world or that which is to come, although the multitude should unceasingly pursue me with its blame.

Whoever has abandoned the treasure of contentment for the treasure of the world, has sold for a very small sum the Egyptian Joseph.

Come, for the measure of this world's workshop will admit a devout man like you or a profligate like me.

On the day of death we may have to confide our woes to wine; for in such an hour we can put trust in no one.

Scat yourself joyously in your corner and see that no man can keep in mind so strange a disaster.

I behold my idol in the hand of the unworthy. It is in this way that heaven requires the service of such an one as I.

But strive you for patience, O my heart, for God will not allow so priceless a ring to remain in the hands of the Evil One!

From the stormy wind of chance it is not possible to see that on this lawn grew once the wild white rose or the red!

The hot breath of the simoom which has passed across this garden, makes it marvellous that the colour of the rose should remain, or the scent of the jessamine.

The spirit of the age is sick! In this misfortune, O Hafiz, where is the understanding of the physician, or the counsel of the sage?

VII

Better than eternal life is union with the Beloved; grant me that, O Lord, for that is best.

She smote me as with a sword, but to none have I revealed it; to conceal the secret of the Beloved from an enemy is best.

Abide, O my heart, a suppliant in her street; according to the proverb: "An abiding fortune is the best."

O devout man, invite me not to Paradise; for the apple of her chin is better than that garden.

It is better to expire at her threshold bearing the brand of her servitude, than to win the sovereignty of the world.

The dust of the rose which my cypress has crushed beneath her foot, is better than the blood-dyed blossom.

In the name of heaven demand of my physician, when shall this helplessness change for the better!

O young man, avert not your head from the counsel of the aged; for the old man's understanding is better than the young man's fortune.

One night the Beloved said to me: "No eye has looked upon a more radiant jewel than the pearl which hangs in my car."

Words from the mouth of the Beloved are jewels; but those which are uttered by Hafiz are the best.

VIII

Blame not, in the purity of your soul, O pious man, the lover of wine, for the sins of others will not be entered to your account.

Whether I be virtuous or sinful, go you your own way, for in the end everyone will reap according to the seed he has sown.

Strive not to make me despair, because of my past, of the compassion of the Eternal: what know you of who will be accounted good or evil behind the veil?

Everyone, whether he is self-denying or self-indulgent, is seeking after the Beloved. Every place may be the shrine of love, whether it be mosque or synagogue.

Even I am not the only outcast from the cell of piety. Even our ancestor Adam allowed Eden to slip from his hand.

If my head touch the threshold of the tavern, let him who understands not say that my head salutes the threshold.

The garden of Paradise is pleasant, but take heed that you count as gain the shade of the willow and the border of the field.

Put no trust in your works, for on that day of Eternity how can you tell what the pen of the Creator has inscribed against your name.

If your aspiration be well, well is your aspiration: if your soul be well, well is your soul.

On the last day, Hafiz, even though the wine cup be in your hand, you may be borne away to Paradise—even from the street of the tavern.

IX

By the enchantment of the puppet of your eye, you child of happy attributes; by the wonder of your down, you marvel of auspicious omens;

By the draught of your ruby mouth; by your colour and fragrance, O spring of beauty and fascination;

By the dust of your path, which is the tent of Hope; by the earth under your foot, which is the envy of clear water;

By your walk, like the gait of the mountain partridge; by your glances, like the eyes of the gazelle;

By the refinement of your nature, and by your breath—the fragrance of the morning! by the odour of your tresses, and perfume grateful as the northern breeze;

By that onyx eye, which is to me the signet seal of my own; by those jewels, which are the pearls of the casket of speech;

By that leaf of your cheek, which is a rosebud of intellect by that garden of graces, which is the home of my dreams;

Hafiz swears that, if you will turn your regards to him, to satisfy you he will sacrifice, not only riches, and all that he possesses, but life itself.

X

Come and throw our ship into the river of wine, throw lamentation and grief into the soul of the old and the young.

O cupbearer! throw me into the ship of wine, as it is said, "Do good and throw it upon water."

I have turned back through mistake from the street of the tavern: kindly throw me back into the path of righteousness.

Bring a cup of that rose-coloured and musk-scented wine; throw sparks of jealousy and envy into the heart of the rose.

Although I am drunk and bad, be kind; cast a glance at this heart, which is bewildered and distressed.

If you want the sun at midnight, throw off the veil from the face of the rose-faced daughter of the vine.

Do not allow me to be buried in the dust on the day of my death; convey me to the tavern and throw me into the cask of wine.

If the heart of Hafiz withdraws its head a hair's breadth from you, seize it, and throw it into your curling locks.

XI

Come, cupbearer, if you have a love of wine, offer not to me anything except wine. Sell in the tavern the prayer carpet; sell, I say, and bring instead a jug of wine.

Come with pain, if through pain comes the healing. Behold, in love both worlds are as nothing.

The mysteries of the heart in the way of love are the voice of the reed and the lamentation of the lute.

A poor and honest beggar in the path of love, is of more value than a thousand Hatim Tais.

A fairy-faced idol only steps forth sultan-like, and a crowd from the city follow her.

Men gaze at that enchanting face; her cheek is stained with the flush of modesty.

How long will Hafiz endure the grief you cause him! how long endure his wounded heart!

XII

Come, for the House of Hope is built on sand: bring wine, for the fabric of life is as weak as the wind.

I am the slave of his will who, under the azure vault, is free from the colour of submission.

Shall I declare what glad message was brought me, last night, when I lay intoxicated in the wine shop, by an angel from the Unseen?

" O far-seeing falcon, whose seat is in the tree of Paradise—not in this sad corner should be your nest.

"For you are sounding the voices of the Ninth Heaven. I cannot imagine why you have fallen into this snare."

I will give you a word of counsel; keep it in your mind, and act upon it, for it is a precept I have preserved in my memory from the Guide of the Path.

"Expect not the fulfilment of promise from this deceitful world, for this hag has been the bride of a thousand lovers."

Let not the zeal of this world cat you up, and let not my counsel depart from you, for I received it from one who had been a wanderer.

Be content with what you have received, and smooth your frowning forehead, for the door of choice is not open either to you or me.

In the smile of the rose is no sign of promise or fidelity. Lament, you loving nightingale, for here is the place of lamentation.

Why, you feeble rhymes, be filled with envy of Hafiz, because God has permitted him to pour forth sweet words and capture all hearts.

XIII

Come hither, cupbearer, for the cup of the tulip is already brimmed with wine. How many uncertain words, and how long these follies!

Abandon your pomp and your pride; for time has beheld wrinkles in the robe of the Csars, and the fall of the crown of Kai.

Be wise; for the bird of the garden is ceaselessly intoxicated. Awake; for the sleep of non-existence follows you closely.

Softly wave, you branch of the youthful spring; never may misfortune overtake you from the blast of the winter's wind!

Trust not in the love of the spheres, or their endearments; woe unto him who imagines himself safe from their wiles!

Tomorrow a draught may be drawn from the river of Paradise, and surrounded by the Houris; but today take delight in the glances of the cupbearer and a cup of wine.

The morning breeze brings back to my memory the covenant of childhood: oh that childhood could bring a balm to banish heaviness from my soul.

Consider not the splendour and royalty of the rose, for the wind will scatter every petal under its feet.

Fill a cup to the memory of Hatim Tai, that we may shut the black book of the misers.

The wine that gave its colour to the crimson blossom casts out in sweat the inmost grace.

Convey the cushions to the garden; for the cypress stands like a slave in attendance, and the reed has girded its loins.

Hark how the musicians of the mead unite in harmony! the melody of harp and lute; the voice of reed and lyre!

O Hafiz, the renown of your enchanting genius has extended to the limits of Egypt and China, and the borders of Rai and Rum!

XIV

Cupbearer, may the day of the festival be to you a joyful one. Let not the promise you have made me escape your memory.

Let the Daughter of the Vine be in attendance; for the breath of my longing has lifted my heart from its heaviness.

I am amazed, that for so many of the days of separation you have severed your heart from your companions!

God be praised that your garden has received no harm from the wind of winter! neither jessamine, nor rose, nor marjoram, or cypress!

May the evil eye be far from you! from that separation your star and your fortune have given you salvation!

The gladness of the assemblies will greet the footsteps of your coming: may every heart which does not wish you joy be a place of wailing!

Hafiz, let not the fellowship of this ark of Noah pass from your hand, or the deluge of chance may bear away your foundations.

XV

From the street of my friend blows soft breeze of the Dawning Year, with whose help, if you wish it, you may light the lamp of your own heart.

If, like the rose, you have a particle of gold in your possession, for Heaven's sake spend it on pleasure! for the cause of the fault of Karun was his desire for gathering gold.

I have wine pure as the soul, yet the Sufi finds fault with it! O Heavens, may no unhappy fate fall for one day on the man of wisdom.

How seek the way which leads to our wishes? By renouncing our wishes. The crown of excellence is renunciation.

I know not why the lamentation of the turtle dove comes from the lip of the stream; perchance, like me, she has a grief both by day and night.

The sweet comrade has forsaken you! sit now in solitude, O taper! for whether you are content or are consumed is equally according to the will of Heaven.

I will speak a word to you behind the veil—"Come forth like the rosebud: for not more than five days delay the coming of the Spring."

In the arrogance of knowledge deny not to yourself the things of pleasure! Come hither, cupbearer,—for to the fool comes the greatest good fortune.

Go your way and revel in wine and pleasure, and renounce hypocrisy! I shall wonder if you can learn of a more excellent way!

Go into the garden, and there steal from the nightingale the secret of love: come to the assembly, and hear from Hafiz how you should sing a song.

XVI

Glad tidings, O my heart! for the morning breeze has returned, and the Hoopoo, the bearer of good news, has come back from the borders of Saba.

Prolong, O bird of the morning, your song, sweet as David's; for the rose, rivalling Solomon, has returned on the wings of the wind.

The tulip has discovered the scent of the wine in the breath of the morning; she bears wounds on her heart, but hopes for a remedy.

Where is the wise man who can speak the speech of the lily, that he may ask her, "Whither she went, and why she has again returned?"

My eyes flowed with tears as they watched the departing caravan, till on the car of my heart again sounded the voice of the camel bell.

Kindness and a happy lot has God vouchsafed to me; for it was God's mercy which restored to me that stony-hearted idol.

Though Hafiz knocked at the door of offence and broke his faith, behold his grace, who came to my door with a message of peace.

XVII

Greetings pleasant as the perfume of friendship to the man whose eye is radiant with light.

Blessings like the light of the pure in heart to the taper which lights the cell of the devout.

I behold no more in his place one who was my companion: my heart is wounded with grief! The cupbearer, where is he?

Where do they sell the wine which overcomes the Sufi? for I am consumed with anger at the hypocrisy of the devotee!

My comrades have so torn the covenant of friendship, that you would imagine that friendship itself had never existed!

Turn not your countenance from the street of the Mage, for there they sell the key which unlocks all difficulties.

The bride of the world, though excelling in loveliness, excels also in the way of deceit.

If my broken heart could attain its wishes, it would not seek its balm from those stony hearts.

Would you master the alchemy of felicity, hold yourself aloof from evil fellowship.

If you will spare me, covetous soul, I shall become many times a king in my need.

Hafiz, complain not of the violence of Time: what know you, slave, of the work of the Master?

XVIII

Grieve not; the lost Yusuf will yet return to Canaan, the cell of sorrow will one day be changed into a rose garden.

Grieve not, you stricken heart, your evil will be changed to good: dwell not upon woe; this bewildered head will return to reason.

Grieve not; if the springtide of life should once more mount the throne of the garden, you will soon, O singer of the night, see above your head a curtain of roses.

Grieve not, because you understand not life's mystery; behind the veil is concealed many a delight.

Grieve not, if for two days the circling sphere revolve not according to our desires; the wheel of time moves not always in one way.

Grieve not, if when through love of the Shrine you set your foot in the desert you are wounded by the thorn.

Grieve not, my soul, if the torrent or mortality upheave the foundation of life, since in the deluge you have Noah for your pilot.

Grieve not; though the journey of life be bitter, and the end unseen, there is no road which does not lead to an end.

Grieve not at the absence of the beloved and at the presence of the enemy: all is known to God, who decrees our fate.

Grieve not, Hafiz, in the corner of poverty, and in the loneliness of dark nights, whilst there remains to you prayer and the reading of the Koran.

XIX

Had I but the power to dwell in your presence, what more could I ask from, my star?

If clamorous adorers surround your threshold, who can wonder? for around the sugar the fly must ever be buzzing.

What need of a sword to slay the lover, when a glance can take from me half my life?

If in both worlds I could breathe a breath with my beloved, that breath would be my gain from both worlds.

Since destiny has so shortened the arm of my desire, how shall I ever attain the height of your lofty cypress?

How shall the drowning wretch discover a way of safety, when the torrent of love has surrounded him before and behind?

If a thousand times I should meet my beloved, the next time she encounters me she will exclaim, "Who is that man?"

Sweet is the coloured wine and the companionship of the beloved. Hafiz, who has lost his heart, will always believe this creed.

XX

Hail, Shiraz! peerless site! Heaven defend it from every danger. Give a hundred praises to our Roknabad, to which the light of Heaven has given its radiance!

For between Jafferabad and Mosella blows his north wind scented with ambergris.

Come you to Shiraz, and the outpouring of the Holy Spirit entreat for it, from the man who is the possessor of perfection.

Let no one vaunt here the sugar of Egypt, for our sweet ones have no cause for shame.

O, morning breeze, what news do you bear of that intoxicated beauty? what tidings can you give me of her state?

O God! awaken me not from my dream, that I may sweeten my loneliness with that vision.

Yes, if that sweet one should wish to shed my blood, yield it up, my heart, like mother's milk.

Wherefore, O Hafiz, if you are overwhelmed by the thought of absence, were you not grateful for the days of the presence of the beloved?

XXI

Heart and faith had departed, and the stealer stood up in wrath and said: "Sit no longer beside me, for safety has abandoned you!"

Have you ever heard of any one who, sitting down at the feast to enjoy his hour, in the end did not rise up repentant and withdraw from its company?

If the tongue of the taper boasted of that laughing face, did it not burn at night in the presence of your adorer?

The breeze of spring in the garden had to tear itself away from the embrace of the rose and the cypress; in vain transported with passionate admiration of your face and form.

You did but pass by in your intoxication, and angels came forth to gaze at you with the tumult of the day of resurrection.

In the presence of your grace the proud cypress stayed its foot in confusion, envying your height and form.

Hafiz! cast your fanatical garment from off you; for there comes forth fire from the garment of hypocrisy.

XXII

Heart-stricken as I am, I have the right of salt upon my mouth; guard you the right, for I depart. God keep you!

You are that pure jewel, the acclaiming of whose excellence might, in the holy world, be the praise of angels.

If you have a doubt of my truth, put it to the test; nothing can try the truth of fine gold like the touchstone.

You have said to me, "I am intoxicated; I will give you two kisses." You have made endless promises, but you gave me neither two kisses nor one kiss.

Open your smiling lips and scatter sweetness around; leave not the people in uncertainty of your mouth.

I will break the spheres to fragments if they wheel not according to my wish; I am not the man to allow myself to he crushed by the sphere of Fate.

If you will not allow her to have access to Hafiz, O my enemy, remove yourself one or two paces from her.

XXIII

Heaven has marvellously vouchsafed its help on this day of judgment! How will you manifest your gratitude? What will be your tribute of thanks?

In the street of love royal splendour has no value; confess the conditions of slavery, and claim your bondage.

Over him who fell, and whom God has held by the hand, say, "Be it your part to share the sorrows of the fallen."

O cupbearer, enter my door with tidings of joy, that for one moment you may drive the woes of the world from my heart.

In the royal road of dignity and grandeur there is much danger; over this uneven way it is well to travel lightly.

The sultan's thoughts are of enemies, of crowns and possessions; the dervish's thoughts are the calm of the heart and the corner of the kalendar.

The attainment of our wishes must be bound by the limit of reflection and determination, with the help of the king's liberality and the grace of God.

I will say to you—if you will allow me—one word of the wise, "Peace is better than war and lordship."

Hafiz, wash not from your face this dust of poverty and peace; for this dust is better than the work of alchemy.

XXIV

She is not the beloved who can only boast of waist and tresses: be the slave of her beauty who is all perfection.

The way of houri and peri is enchanting; but there is one who is fairest and rarest.

O smiling rose, approach the fountain of my eye, which in the hope of you fills with sweet water.

The curve of your eyebrows takes, with an archer's craft, the weapon from the hand of all who hold the bow.

My words must soothe the heart since you do accept them: in truth all words of love make an impression.

In the path of love none have been wholly initiated into the mystery; everyone forms his judgment according to his understanding.

Boast not of your generosity amongst the frequenters of the tavern: every word has its time; every subtlety its place.

Since autumn comes close on the track of the spring, the wise bird will not go forth in the meadow singing its song.

Who bears off from you the ball of beauty, when even the sun is a rider who at times has not the bridle in his hand.

Say to the rival,—"Try not your wit and your subtlety on Hafiz, for my reed has also its tongue and its meaning!"

XXV

He who enriched your cheek with the bloom of the rose and the wild rose, can give to me, most miserable, patience and rest.

And he who gave your tresses the gift of length is also able, in his mercy, to give some gift to me.

I abandoned all my hopes of Ferhad on that day when he gave the reins of his ruined heart to the lips of Shirin.

If I do not own a treasure of gold, contentment yet remains to me: he who gave that to kings, has also given this to beggars.

The world is a beautiful bride to behold, but he who has betrothed her has given his life for her dowry.

Henceforward I will take my pleasure in the cypress and the lip of the stream—the more, that now the breeze bears to me glad tidings of the return of February.

In the hand of sorrow the heart of Hafiz ran blood: atone for severance from your support, O Support of The Faith.

XXVI

How well a sweet verse can comfort a heavy heart! A subtle utterance from the book of my songs would be of this strain!

Could I discover in your crimson lip a ring of protection, I would sway, like Solomon, a hundred kingdoms by my seal!

It is not well, O my heart, to be weighed down with sorrow through the stab of envy; perchance when you look at it again it may seem to be good.

As for him who does not understand my imaginative reed, let his pictures perish, though he were a painter from China.

Each one has his gift—one a cup of wine, another the heart's blood: such are the laws of the circle of destiny.

In the matter of roses and rose water this is the decree—that the rose should be shown in the market, and that the rose water should remain behind the veil.

It cannot be that the love of revelling will abandon the heart of Hafiz, for the habit of earlier days will last till the later days.

XXVII

I am a stranger, and you are courteous to strangers. Spend a moment on the condition of your stranger.

Bind me by whatsoever noose you like, provided you do not take back your face from my sight.

I kiss the threshold of the thought of union, since the hand of supplication has no power to touch your sleeve.

I, a wretched man, do not place my face on your threshold for the first time; nay, I placed it there from time without beginning.

My heart! do not complain of the evening, for the morning comes after it; even as sting and honey, and descent and ascent, come together.

If you make me like the dust of the ground, continue to cast your shadow on that dust.

The heart of my heart complains like the dove. What fire is it, that you have cast on my life?

My heart thinks of your tall stature and my short arm.

O my enemy, the tale of my grief is not of today; nay, Hafiz from time without beginning was a drunkard and a profligate.

XXVIII

I am the lover of my love: what have I to do with faith and unfaith? I am thirsty of pain: what have I to do with union and disunion?

If I do not find life on the lip of the beloved, what have I to do with that life which is without the beloved?

If I am killed by love, what need I fear from the sword of the sultan?

I am a naked, needy man: what business have I with the treasuries of kings?

The eyebrow of the beloved alone is my Mecca: what has this distracted heart to do with the Place of the Pilgrimage?

Were I to want the beloved in this world, what should I care for Paradise and its changeless maidens?

Whosoever lost himself in the path of love, what knowledge has he of grief and pain, and what has he to do with remedy?

O Hafiz! if you are a lover and a drunkard, say once more, "I am the lover of the beloved, what have I to do with faith and unfaith?"

XXIX

I am he who has opened his eye to see the beloved. O sovereign, kind to your slaves! how can I thank you?

Tell him who is needy and troubled not to wash his face clean of dust, because the dust of the street of supplication is the elixir of desire.

In return for a tear or two which you shed, O eye, how many glances do you cast on the face of prosperity.

If the lover does not perform his ablutions with the blood of his heart, according to the word of the judge of love, his prayer does not prosper.

From the difficulties of the path, O heart! do not turn the rein, for the traveller should not think of descent and ascent.

In this fantastic abode take nothing but the cup; in this House of Illusion do not play any game but love.

What gain can I get from the tale-bearing breeze, when the straight cypress in this garden is not a confidant?

Although your beauty is independent of love, I am not the one who will turn back from this love game.

The singing of another cannot prevail in that place where Hafiz raises his voice.

XXX

I complain every moment of the hand of separation. I weep if the wind does not carry the sound of my sighing to you.

What can I do, save weep, because from your absence I am in such case as I would have your evil-wisher to share.

Day and night I drink tears and blood. Why should I not, since I am far from your sight? How could I be glad at heart?

Since you went far from me, the broken-hearted, what tears of blood has the heart poured forth!

From the end of every eyelash dropped countless drops of blood, when the heart made complaint against the hand of separation.

Unhappy Hafiz is drowned in your remembrance day and night, but you are heedless of your broken-hearted slave.

XXXI

I do not see friendship any more. When did friendship come to an end? What has become of the companions?

The water of life became darkened: where is auspicious-footed Khizr? Blood runs from the branch of the rose: what word of the wind of spring?

Thousands of roses blossom, and the song of not a single bird is heard. What has become of the nightingales?

It is years since a royal ruby came from the mine of humanity. What has become of the heat of the sun, and of the travail of the cloud and rain?

Love does not touch the lyre: is that harp burnt? No one has a lust for drunkenness: what has befallen winedrinkers?

Who says that friends observe the due of friendship: what has become of the grateful; what has become of friends?

The ball of divine grace and munificence is thrown on the ground. No one appears in the field: what has become of the horsemen?

Hafiz! no one knows the secrets of God. Be silent. Why do you ask what happens in the whirl of Time?

XXXII

If at the song of the turtle dove and the nightingale you will not drink wine, how can I heal you, save by the final remedy burning!

When the rose has flung aside her veil, and the bird is singing his song, cast not the cup from your hand! What signifies your lamentation!

Whilst the water of life is within your reach, expire not of thirst! "Water gives life to all things."

Gather treasures for yourself from the colours and odours of springtide, for the autumn and the winter follow fast upon its heels.

Fate gives no gift which it snatches not again: demand nothing of poor humanity; the gift it gives is of no value.

How should the pomp of majesty and power be abiding? Of the throne of Jamshid, the crown of Kai, what remains but a tale!

He who hoards up wealth to be the heritage of the worthless is an infidel; so says the singer, so says the cupbearer; such is the law of the lute and the lyre!

It is graven on the gate of the House of Heaven,—" Woe to him who has bought the smiles of the world."

Generosity has withered away! I seal up my lips. Where is the wine, that I may drink this toast: "May the soul of Hatim Tai live in joy for ever!"

The miser will never taste the happiness of Heaven! Come, Hafiz, take the cup and practise generosity, and I will be your surety!

XXXIII

If from your garden I gathered a handful of flowers, what matter? If before the glory of your lamp I bent my looks to my feet, what matter?

O Lord, if I, a sun-stained man, rested a moment beneath the shadow of that tall cypress, what matter?

O seal of Jamshid, of mighty memories, if a gleam from you should be cast upon my ring, what matter?

If Wisdom has departed from its dwelling, and if this wine be the cause of calamity in the House of Faith, what matter?

The devout man woos the favour of the king: if I value more the fascination of a fair image, what matter?

My life has varied between wine and my beloved: if ill have chanced to me from one or from the other, what matter?

The Master knew that I was a lover and kept silence; and if Hafiz knows it likewise, what matter?

XXXIV

If my heart draws me to the musk-scented grape, so be it! From austerity and hypocrisy comes no sweet smell.

Were all the world to prohibit love, I would still obey that Lord's decrees.

Let no greed prevent you from the promptings of—generosity, for the generous forgive the faults and pardon the lover.

My heart continues unmoved within the circle of prayer, and hopes thereby to attain a lock from the tresses of the loved one.

To you whom Heaven has vouchsafed beauty and the chamber of fortune, what do you want of the tirewoman to attire you?

The meadow is fair, and the breeze heart-enrapturing, and the wine pure: what is wanting now, except a contented heart?

The world is a bride of surpassing beauty—but remember that this maiden is never bound to anyone.

The field is never wholly void of cypress and tulip; one goes, but another yet appears in its place.

It is not necessary to question the heart about our wretched condition; for the mirror of the face reflects all things.

I said to her playfully, "Ah! face fair as the moon, why will you not bestow on me, the broken-hearted, one morsel of sugar for my balm?"

Laughing she answered, "Heaven forbid, Hafiz, that kiss of your should profane my moon-fair face!"

XXXV

If that angel of Shiraz would take my heart in hand, I would give for her dark mole Samarkand and Bokhara.

Saki, bring me the wine that remains, for in Paradise you will not see the marge of the water of Roknabad, nor the rose garden of our Mosella.

Alas! those wanton ones, those fair disturbers of our city, bear patience from my heart as Turkomans their plunder.

Yet the beauty of the beloved has no need of our imperfect love!—To a lovely face what need is there of paint or powder, of mole or dye

Tell to me the tale of the musician and of wine, and search less into the secrets of time; for none in their wisdom have ever solved, or will ever solve, that mystery.

I can, understand how the beauty of Yusuf, waxing day by day, lured Zulaikha from the veil of her modesty.

You have spoken ill of me, and I am happy:—God pardon you!—You have spoken well; for even a bitter word is welcome when it falls from a sweet honey lip.

O, my soul, hearken to good counsel, for noble youths love the teaching of the Sage more than their own souls.

You have rhymed your ghazel: you have strung your pearls. Come, O Hafiz, and sing it sweetly—that Heaven may shed upon your song the glory of the Pleiades.

XXXVI

If the hand of your musk-scented tresses has sinned against me, and if the dark mole of your cheek has been heartless to me, gone is gone!

If the lightning of love has destroyed the harvest of the poor wool-garbed dervish, or if the tyranny of a mighty king has injured the beggar, gone is gone!

If a heart has been oppressed by the glance of the beloved who has it in keeping, or if anything has marred the concord between lover and loved one, gone is gone!

If complaints have been spread abroad by the tale-hearers, or if among comrades anything unfitting has been spoken, gone is gone!

On the highway of love should be no heart-burning:—bring me wine! When anything that was impure has become pure again, gone is gone!

In the game of love, patience is needful:—be strong, my heart! If there was heart pain, if there was cruelty, gone is gone!

O preacher, be not eloquent on the backslidings of Hafiz, who has escaped from the cloister. Who shall bind the foot of the freeman? Gone is gone!

XXXVI

If I live I shall go once more to the wine house. I shall do nothing but serve the profligate.

Happy the day on which I go with weeping eyes, so that I may once more sprinkle water on the wine house door.

There is no wisdom in this tribe. 0 God ! help, so that I may carry my own jewel to another purchaser.

My heart wants ease, if the blandishments, if the tresses of the beloved any more allow it.

If the circle of the blue sphere may be my helper, I shall bring the beloved once more to another circle.

See our hidden secret, which is told in
song, with drum and lute, at the head of another market.

If the beloved went away and did not recognize the right of old acquaintance, God forbid that I should go in pursuit of another beloved.

Every moment I cry with grief that the sky every moment seeks to injure more my distressed heart.

I say again, that Hafiz alone is not in this misfortune. A great many more are lost in this desert.

XXXVIII

If your face is compared with the moon and the Pleiades, it is compared by guesswork, your face not being seen.

Those tales which are told of Farhad and Shirin are a part of the tale of our tumult-exciting love.

The dust of the street of the winners of hearts possesses life-giving odour: lovers have found the perfume of wisdom in that place.

The earth-stained are without a draught from the cup of generosity. Sec what oppression is practised upon poor lovers.

The longest feather in the wing of the crow and the kite is not fit for hunt and chase, because this grace is given to the noblest bird, the royal white falcon.

O cupbearer, pour wine, because there is no fighting against the order of original destiny. Whatever is destined may not be changed.

Be no stranger to wisdom; draw into your arms the daughter of the vine, to whom is given, as marriage portion, the dowry of wisdom.

Do not look with contempt at the earthen cup of the profligate, for these companions have served the world-seeing cup.

The arrows of eyelashes and glances of magic did not do that which those ringlets and that mole have done.

One kiss was our reward, and your lip did not give it; you yourself owe me justice. The sweet-lipped should do this.

The beloved, with the fire of their fair cheeks, every moment have made breaches into the heart and faith of the pious.

Wherever the poem of Hafiz, which is from end to end the praise of your beauty, is heard, it is praised by the truthful.

XXXIX

I gazed upon the heavens, spread out like a green field, and at the sickle of the new moon, and I thought of my own cornfields and the time of harvest.

And I exclaimed: "O Fortune, the sun has risen, and you have lost yourself in sleep." And Fortune replied: "Notwithstanding all that has befallen, despair not!"

If you will raise yourself undefiled and naked to heaven like the Messiah, from your splendour many rays will yet go upward towards the sun.

Put no trust in the stars, those midnight thieves, for they have stolen away the crown of Kaus, and the girdle of Kai-Khosru.

O Heaven! demand not so great a price for your glory; for in love the harvest of the moon is sold for one barleycorn, and the cluster of the Pleiades for two barleycorns.

Though an earring of gold and ruby weigh down your car, the abiding of beauty is brief: give ear to wise counsel.

Far be the evil eye from the mole on your cheek! for on the chessboard of beauty the pawn it advanced forward has gained the stakes from sun and moon.

The flame of hypocrisy and deceit will consume the harvest of religion. O Hafiz throw aside your woolen garment, and go your way.

XL

I give you advice; hear it, and do not seek an excuse. Accept what the kind counsellor tells you.

Take advantage of union with those of youthful face, because in the ambush of life is the deceit of the old world.

The affluence of both the worlds is as a barleycorn before lovers, because the one is a little thing, and the other a trifle.

I want a pleasant friend, and music with an instrument, so that I may give out my grief with bass and treble tone.

I am resolved that I will not drink wine, and will not commit sin, if fate prop my purpose.

Who would hinder our horror-stricken heart? Inform Majnun who is freed from fetters.

Since eternal fate was made without my presence, if in a little I at3 not according to the law, do not blame.

I often put aside the cup with the purpose of repentance, but the glance of the cupbearer does not encourage me.

O cupbearer! pour into my cup pure wine like the tulip, that the thought of the mole of my beloved may not go away from my mind.

Wine two years old, and the beloved fourteen years old, are all the company of the little and the great to me.

Did I not tell you, O heart! to abstain from her tresses, in whose noose the very wind is held!

Bring the ruby cup of grace and pearl. Tell the jealous one, "See the generosity of an Asaf and die."

Drink wine, and make resolve of union with the beloved: hear the word that is cried to you from the ninth heaven.

Hafiz, do not tell, at this banquet, your tale of vowing to sin no more, otherwise the cupbearers with the arched eyebrows will strike you with arrows.

What worth have the sayings of Khaju and the poems of Sulaiman? Nay, better than the verse of Zahir is the verse of Hafiz.

XLI

I heard a sweet saying which was I uttered by the old man of Canaan: "No tongue can express the sorrow of separation from the beloved!"

The words of the preacher proclaiming to the city the dread tale of the day of resurrection are but a description of the day of separation.

From whom shall I demand a token of the departed beloved? For whatsoever the wind said, the words of the wind have perished.

Warm the old grief with old wine, for this is the saying of the head of the village, "Wine is the seed to bring forth a harvest of happiness."

Alas! that to that unkind moon, the friend of my enemy, it has been so easy to abandon the companionship of the loving ones!

From henceforth I give up my mind to contentment, thanks to my rival; for my heart has become accustomed to grief, and will no longer seek for medicine.

Hope not to hold the wind, though it blow in the way of your wishes; for the wind itself once gave this proverb to Solomon.

Though Fate seem to grant you a grace, turn you not from the path: for who has assured you that the hag has said farewell to her falsehoods?

Utter no word concerning the How and the Why, for the faithful slave accepts with his soul the speech of the Sultan.

Who has said that Hafiz has recalled one thought from you? I have never said so, and if anyone has said so he has spoken slander!

XLII

I have made a compact with the beloved of my soul, that while I have a soul within my body I will esteem as my own soul the well wishers of her street.

In the core of my heart I get light from that taper of Chigil: glory comes to my eye and lustre to my heart from that moon of Khutan.

Since I have won the desires and wishes of my heart, what need I care for the venom of evil speakers in the crowd!

If a hundred armies of beauties should lie in ambush to attack my heart, I have, by the mercy of Heaven, an idol which will shatter their armies.

Would to Heaven, O watcher, that you would shut your eye this night for a time, that I might murmur a hundred words on her silent ruby lips!

No desire have I for tulip, or wild white rose, or narcissus, so long as, by Heaven's mercy, I walk proudly in the rose garden of her favour.

O ancient of wisdom, lay not your curse on the tavern; for in renouncing the wine cup I should break a promise to my heart.

My drink is sweet of savour, and my beloved is fair as a picture: no one has a beloved like my beloved.

I have a cypress in my dwelling, under the shadow of whose stature I can forget the cypress of the garden, and the box tree of the lawn.

I can boast that the seal of her ruby mouth is as powerful as the seal of Solomon: having the Great Name, why should I fear the Evil One?

After long abstinence, Hafiz became a renowned

reveller; but why need I grieve, while I have in the world a protector?

XLIII

I laid my face in her path, but she came not nigh me: I longed for a hundred greetings, but she vouchsafed me not one glance.

O Lord, protect that young heartless beauty from the arrows of the sighs of her lovers.

The torrent of my tears has not washed away malice from her heart; no rain drop has made an impression on that hard stone.

Would that, like a taper, I might die under her feet; but she will not pass by me like the morning breeze.

O soul, what heart of stone is so pulseless that it would not shield itself against the wound of your arrow!

My lamenting last night allowed no fowl or fish to sleep; but behold, that scornful one never unclosed her eyelids.

Your sweet song, O Hafiz, is so heart-enthralling, that all who hear it desire to hold it in their hearts.

XLIV

In none can I find friendship: what has become of those who were my friends? How has friendship ended? Where are those gone who were my friends?

The fountain of life is disturbed: whither has the auspicious friend Khisar departed? The rose has lost its colour. What is become of the spring breeze?

No one can say he has a friend who possesses the right of friendship: what has come to those who trusted in friendship? Where are their friends gone?

The ball of good luck and of fair fortune has been cast into the midst of the field, but no one has come forth upon the plain: what has become of the horsemen?

Thousands of roses have bloomed, but no song of a bird has arisen: whither are the nightingales gone? What has become of the thousand-voiced singers?

Zuhra no more plays her tuneful melodies: has she perhaps burnt her lute? No one delights in the joy of the grapejuice: what has happened to the winedrinkers?

This land was once named "The City of Friends," "The Place of Loved Ones." How has friendship ceased utterly? What has become of the friends of the city?

No ruby has been produced from the mine of manhood for many a year: the heat of the sun, the strength of the wind and the rain, whither are they gone?

No one has knowledge of the divine mysteries; therefore be silent O Hafiz: for of whom will you inquire what will chance to the wheel of Time?

XLV

In the city there is no beloved who can win my heart. If Fortune is my friend, let it carry my chattels from this place.

Where is the happy and merry-making comrade, before whose kindness the broken-hearted lover may describe his desire?

In my imagination I play all this game, in the hope that, perhaps, a master of vision might wish to see it.

Although the path of love is the ambush of archers, whosoever goes craftily gains victory over the enemies.

Magic cannot compete with miracle; keep up your heart. Who is the enemy that may excel the miracle?

The cup of wine stays the flood of sorrow. Do not give it up from your hand, or the flood of sorrow will drown you.

O gardener, I see you are heedless or autumn: I pity that day on which the wind withers your beautiful rose!

The highwayman, Time, is not asleep, do not be secure from him: if he has not taken you today, surely tomorrow he will take you.

When the bellowing of the bull gives back echo, the ass is cheated: how can a star steal the reflection of the brilliant sun?

The narcissus eyes of the beloved will, I am afraid, take away at once that knowledge and wisdom which my heart collected for forty years.

Hafiz, if the eyes of the beloved seek your life, open the house of life and quit it, so that her eyes may carry your life away.

XLVI

In the dawn of the morning I confided to the breeze the story of my longings; and it returned tome a response: "Have faith in the compassion of the Lord."

Words have no language which can utter the secrets of love; and beyond the limits of expression is the expounding of desire.

Tie your heart to the tresses of Laila, and do your deeds after the example of Majnun; for words of wisdom are considered a folly by the lover.

O you, my Yusuf of Egypt engaged with rulership, inquire of the father—"What bounds are there to the love of the child?"

Throw upon us the enchantment of one of your glances, at the same moment bringing the balm and making the wound: let us touch those musk-exhaling tresses, at once heart-soothing and heart-enthralling.

The world, at the same time old and lovely, never yet contained compassion in her nature: what do you hope from her affection? why do you ask from her the assuagement of your longing?

The profit of the marketplace is solely for the Sage. Make me happy, High Heaven, with the Wisdom of the Wise.

The prayer of the morning and the supplication of the evening are the key to your Treasure-House. Travel by the true path if you would be with the Beloved.

How long shall a man like you lust after the bones of greed? Why do you cast the shadow of fortune on the unworthy?

Waste not your heart on wantons, Hafiz. Behold how

faithless were the fair girls of Samarkand to their lovers.

Dance, dance to the singing of Hafiz of Shiraz, you dark-eyed daughters of Kashmir, you fair girls of Samarkand.

XLVII

In the dawn of the morning, when from the hidden halls of the House of Wonders the torch of the east throws its rays on every side;

When the sky draws forth its mirror from the horizon, and exhibits the face of the Universe in a thousand ways;

When from the hidden halls of the House of Joy, wherein dwells the Jamshid of Heaven, Zuhra tunes her organ to the music of the spheres;

Then is the lute inspired to exclaim—"Who is he who denies?" and the cup laughingly to respond—"Where is he who refuses?"

Consider the movements of the revolving sphere, and clutch the cup of pleasure; for in every condition this is the wisest way.

The tresses, of the Queen of the world are a vanity and a deception; the most wise will not seek the end of those threads.

Pray for the life of the king, if you desire the profit of the world; for it is a life generous, great, benevolent.

An image of eternal grace, brilliant as the eye of hope, the sum of all knowledge and action, the soul of the world, such is the King!

O Hafiz, like a slave be an abider at his threshold; for he is an obedient King, and Lord of those who are obeyed.

XLVIII

In the dawn the bird of the garden spoke to the rose: "Be not so disdainful, for in this garden many like you have blossomed."

The rose smiled, and replied: "We do not weep at the truth, but no lover would speak harshly to the loved one!"

To all eternity the perfume of love will be unknown to the man who has never swept with his forehead the dust from the threshold of the tavern.

If you desire to drink red wine from that jewelled cup, then you must pierce many a pearl with the point of your eyelashes!

Yesterday, when in the garden of Iam the morning breeze with its boon breath began to ruffle the hair of the hyacinth.

I cried, "O throne of Jamshid, where is your world-displaying cup?" and it replied, "Alas! that watchful fate should have slept!"

The speech of love is not that which comes to the tongue. O cupbearer, cut short this questioning and answering.

The tears of Hafiz have thrown endurance and wisdom into the sea. How could he do otherwise? How could he hide the consuming torments of love?

XLIX

In the magic mirror of the cup behold, O Sufi, the splendour of red wine. Seek among the drinkers of wine for the mystery behind the veil; for that mystery belongs not to the renowned in religion.

The dragon is not the prey of any man; draw in your nets, for here nothing save the wind is caught in your snares.

Live in the living hour, for Fortune is fickle. Was not Adam cast forth from the gardens of Paradise?

At the feast of life drink a round or twain and depart, for truly it were vain to wish for enduring delight.

Soul, my soul, your youth has vanished and you did not pluck the rose of life. Use now the hours of your age in virtue, loyalty, and honour.

Hafiz thirsts for a cup of wine; fly hence, O zephyr, and from the slave present respects to the master.

L

When in the midst of prayer came memory of your arched eyebrows, it struck so deep that the very shrine lamented.

Expel from me patience of heart or mind no longer; for that patience you perceive in me was borne only on the wind.

The wine is clear, the birds of the meadow are intoxicated: it is the season of love, and life is on a fair foundation.

The rose has brought its beauty, and the soft wind its gladness, and from all parts comes an odour of healthfulness.

O bride of Virtue, reproach not destiny; prepare the fair bridal chamber, for the bridegroom is coming.

The heart-enthralling blossoms are decked in all their jewels, but our beloved comes in the beauty of the Lord.

Every tree that brings forth fruit bends beneath its burden: ah! fortunate cypress, which are free from the weight of grief.

Minstrel, sing a sweet verse from the songs of Hafiz, that I may exclaim—" It brings back to my memory the time of joy!"

LI

In the morning I strayed to the garden, drawn by the scent of the roses, that, like the desolate nightingale, I might find balm for my brain.

I gazed on the face of a red rose, which lit the darkness of the night like a lamp.

So proud was she of her own youth and beauty, that she banished all repose from the heart of the melodious nightingale.

The eye of the exquisite narcissus was filled with tears from compassion: the tulip in her grief displayed a hundred wounds in her heart and soul.

The lily thrust forth her tongue in reproof like a sword: the anemone opened her mouth like a gossip.

Now with flagon in hand, be like drinkers of wine! now like cupbearers minister to the drinkers with cup in hand.

Count gaiety and pleasure, youth, as plunder, like the rose: for, Hafiz, the messenger has no more to do than deliver his message.

LII

In good sooth, O Saki, bear round the wine and present the beaker. For love at first seemed delightful, but since then difficulties have arisen.

In the hope of the balm which the breezes shall bear from that forehead, from the flow of her musk-scented tresses, the hot blood fills our hearts.

Stain the very prayer carpet with wine if the Host of the House command you; for the traveller should be aware of the ways of the stages of travel.

Where is my leisure for love in the home of the loved one, when at every moment the bell booms forth the signal to bind on the burden?

While we fear the blackness of the night and the wildness of the waves and the whirlpool, what can those know of our case who bear light burdens on the shore?

All my deliberate deeds have earned me an evil name. How can the mystery remain secret which is babbled of in the assembly?

If you long for peace scorn not this counsel, Hafiz: when you shalt hold the beloved say farewell to the world and abandon it.

LIII

Is there anything dearer than the beauty of the garden and the presence of spring? But where is the cupbearer? Say, what is the reason that he tarries?

Every happy moment that comes in your way, treasure as a prize! Let no one delay, for who knows what the end will be?

The bond of life is but a single hair! Use your intelligence, be your own friend in trouble, and what then is your injury?

The meaning of the Water of Life, and the Garden of Iram, what is it but the delight of a stream and the delight of wine?

The austere man and the profligate are both of one tribe; what is there to choose between them that we should give up our souls to either?

What do the silent heavens reveal of the secret behind the veil? O arguer, why strive with the keeper of the veil!

If for the slave who is wrapped up in error or in ignorance there is no celestial justice, what is the meaning of the words pardon, and the mercy of the All Powerful?

The devotee thirsts for the wine of Kausar, and Hafiz for the wine of life. Between these two, what is the choice of the Creator?

LIV

It is a holiday, and the rose and friends are in expectation. O cupbearer! see the moon in the face of the king and bring wine.

I had withdrawn my heart from the time of the rose, but the blessings of the pure of the age did little.

It the morning meal is lost, what matter? there is still the morning wine. Seekers after the beloved break their fast with wine.

Save the money of life, I have nothing in my hand. Where is wine, that I may offer that also to the beauty of the cupbearer?

Fortune is good and pleasant, and pleasant the generous king. God guard each of these from the wound of Time.

Drink wine to my song, because your jewelled cup will give a different taste to this royal pearl.

Do not set your heart upon the world, and ask of the drunkard the grace of the cup, and the story of Jamshid.

O heart! the majesty of love is great. Resolve. Hear well the story; listen to the tale.

As it is your universal kindness to offer a veil, cover our heart, which is as coin alloyed below the standard.

I fear that, on the day of judgment, the rosary of the sage and the rag of the wine-drinking profligate will be equal.

O Hafiz! since the fast day has passed off, and the rose also goes away, being helpless, drink wine, because opportunity is lost to your hand.

LV

It is the night of power, and the book of separation is closed. There is safety in that night till the rising of the morn!

O heart! be firm-footed in love, because in this path no work is without a reward.

I will not repent of my profligacy, although you may injure me by separation and by absence.

My heart left my hand, yet I did not see the face of the beloved. Alas for this tyranny, and woe for this cruelty!

Come up, O bright-minded morning! for I see that the night of separation is extremely dark.

If you want faithfulness, be an endurer of the tyranny of the beloved, O Hafiz! Indeed there are profit and loss in the traffic of love.

LVI

It is the fresh spring! Strive to be of joyous heart, for it will see many roses when you shalt lie beneath the earth.

The harp behind the veil might give instruction to your heart, but its warning can only avail if you shalt be able to hear it.

I will not tell you now with whom to consort, nor what to drink, for you are yourself aware, if you be learned and prudent, what you should do.

Every leaf in the field is a volume of a different kind: it were evil to you if you could be unmindful of them all.

Although the road which leads from us to the Friend be beset with dangers, yet the journey will be easy if you have knowledge of the stages.

The clutch of the world takes away too much of the money of your life, if by day and night you are absorbed in this difficult problem.

O Hafiz! if high fortune shall honour you with help, you will yet become the spoil of that excelling beauty.

LVII

I went forth into the garden to gather the rose of the morning, when on a sudden sounded in my ears the song of the nightingale.

Unhappy as myself, tortured with his passion for the rose, he filled the sward with the voice of his wailing.

Long I paced the walks of the garden, considering the case of the rose and the nightingale:

The rose became the friend of the thorn, while the nightingale was still the constant lover. The one is ever unaltered, the other is changeful.

The voice of the nightingale pierced my heart, until I was so stirred, that I lost all power of patience.

Many a rose has bloomed in this garden, yet no one has plucked a rose without being wounded by its thorn!

O Hafiz! cherish no hope of happiness in this world; for with its thousand imperfections it can display no perfect excellence.

LVIII

Last night a man of wisdom said to me: The secret of the wineseller must no longer be hidden from you.

Then he continued—"Take matters upon yourself lightly, for it is the way of the world to lay burdens on him who is ready to do hard work."

Then he delivered into my hand a cup, which reflected the glory of Heaven so brilliantly, that Zuhrah began dancing, and the lute player said—"Drink."

Give ear unto my counsel, O my son, and trouble not yourself about the things of this world: I will bestow on you words like pearls, if you can hear them.

Take life, like this cup, with a laughing lip, even though with a bleeding heart: nor even if you are wounded lament like a lute.

Till you have penetrated behind the veil, you will hear nothing. The ear of the uninitiated cannot receive an angel's message.

In the House of Love, boast not of question and answer; for there every limb must be wholly eye and ear.

On the carpet of the subtle there is no place for self praise; either speak words of weight, man of wisdom, or remain silent!

Cupbearer, bring me wine; for the follies of Hafiz have been understood by the Lord of gladness, the forgiver of sins, the blotter out of errors.

LIX

Let no one be vexed like me, the afflicted one, by absence, for all my life has been passed in the pain of separation.

A stranger, a lover, despairing, poor, and distracted, I drag on my days in the sadness of separation.

If he is delivered into my hands I will slay Separation; I will repay with tears the blood money of Separation.

Where shall I go? To whom shall I relate the story of my heart? Who will do me justice? Who will requite me as I deserve for the sorrows of separation?

I will harass Separation, by separation from you: I will make the blood flow from the eyes of Separation.

Whence am I? Whence separation, and whence sorrow? Did my mother bring me forth only to endure separation!

For this cause, with the stigma of love, by night and day, like Hafiz, I answer the morning nightingale with sobs of separation.

LX

May it be remembered that you gave grace to us in secret. The inscription of your love was written on our face.

May it be remembered that when your eyes were reproving me, the miracle of Heaven was on your sugared lip.

May it be remembered that when my moon went, the new moon must needs follow her.

May it be remembered that your face once lit the candle of delight, and lured this heart like a butterfly.

May it be remembered that when, like the smiling cup, you smiled, there were kisses between my lips and your lips.

May it be remembered that, in the House of Happiness, that which smiled on a reveller was red wine.

May it be remembered that those who drank of that wine were none but I and the beloved, and Love was with us.

May it be remembered that I have sat in the tavern and drunk deep. That which is rare in my life nowadays was frequent then.

May it be remembered that, by your help, the poem, the unpierced pearl of Hafiz, was strung.

LXI

May your beauty ever increase! may your tulip-tinted cheek bloom year by year!

May the vision of your love, which is enshrined in my brain, wax stronger every day!

May the forms of all fair women in the world bend ever to the service of your beauty!

May every cypress that grows in our meads be bowed before your stately figure!

May the eye which is not enchanted by you shed blood in place of tears!

May your glance, that it may enthrall every heart, be gifted with all enchantments!

Does a heart exist which would cause your sorrow, may it be deprived of endurance, rest, and peace!

May your crimson lip, dear to Hafiz as his soul, be ever far from the lips of the base and the unworthy!

LXII

My life seems ended, but my desire is not fulfilled; my fortune is not set free from sleep.

The hours of life pass away in this thought, and still the wounds of your tresses do not heal.

My heart became snared in your ringlets, inasmuch as it saw a pleasant territory, and no news comes again of that lost heart.

So long as I do not hold in my arms your fair body, the rose-tree of my heart's desire will not flower.

From the book of sincerity I recalled a thousand words of blessing; not a single one of them is effectual.

I long to speak to the morning breeze about my heart, but the dawn does not come to my window.

The first condition of fidelity is to surrender the heart. Hafiz! go hence if this cannot be done by you.

LXIII

My desire is not yet won from the kiss of your lip. In the hope of that cup of ruby I still live.

In the night of your tresses my heart was lost: what will become of me in the end of this love?

One night I spoke of your hair as the musk of Tartary: that hair still pierces my body every moment with its arrows.

One day my name came to the lip of the beloved: the joy of life yet comes to the wise from my name.

The sun bears the reflection of your face into my rooms: it haunts the shadows on my terrace.

From the dawn of time the cupbearer of your lip has poured a draught from the cup, for the love of which I still burn.

O cupbearer! give me to drink of that fire-coloured wine, because I am a stranger amongst those who are perfect in love.

O you! who said, "Yield up life, so that you may win peace of mind": I confided my life to her, and still have I no peace.

Hafiz, write the glory of her crimson lip, while the water of life flows from your pen.

LXIV

My heart is overflowing with pain: who will bring me any cure? My heart in its desolation is nigh unto death: who will bestow on me a comrade?

Who longs for an hour of repose from the bitter-visaged world? Cupbearer, bring me a cup, that I may dream in a moment's peace.

Arise, that we may bestow our hearts on those gracious girls of Samarkand; for the breeze bears to us odours from the river Oxus.

I said to a man of wit, "Look upon this my state!" He made answer, "Truly our case is hard, our state is strange; the world is a ruin!"

I am consumed in a pit of patience, because of the beloved! The king of Turkistan regards not my case. Where is the hero Rustum?

In the way of love, suffering is safety and delight: may the heart that would heal a wound, itself be wounded!

To the street of the drunken there is no way for the gentle and kindly: there are snares for the wayfarer, and woes for the unwary!

In the world of dust there is no true man! We must mould another world, we must make a new Adam!

O Hafiz! what are tears, when weighed against love: in this deluge the Seven Seas are accounted as a little night dew.

LXV

My weeping eyes are wet with tears of blood! Behold to what case those who seek after you are brought.

When the sun of your beauty arises on the east of my street, it draws on a day auspicious to my happiness.

The speech of Farhad is the story of Shirin's lip; the braids of Laila's tresses are the dwelling of Majnun.

Be compassionate to my heart, for it is the slave of that cypress-slender body! Speak to me, for your words are gracious and musical.

O Saki with the circling wine, bring solace to my soul; for the hurt of the heart comes from the sorrow of the revolving sphere.

Since the time when that enchanting beloved escaped from my hand, the skirt of my garment has been like the river Jihin.

How can my sad soul become gladsome, when the power of joy is denied by the Power!

Hafiz roams about distracted, seeking the beloved; like to the beggar who seeks for the treasure of Karin.

LXVI

Musselmans, I had once a friend, in whom I could confide every trouble.

A heart that could share in every grief, and a friend who could aid me in every difficulty.

To me, when agitated by any calamity, a comrade both experienced and wise.

When my weeping eye drew me into a whirlpool, my hope of the shore lay in him.

When I wandered in the paths of love, when love clung to my garment, I lost my friend.

In my endeavour to find him my tears fell like pearls, but my efforts to regain his companionship were vain.

There is no skill which is secure from the danger of disappointment, but when was beggar so disappointed as I!

In this hopeless intoxication have compassion on me, who was once a wise and skilful man.

When my words were inspired by love, they were praised for their wisdom in every assembly.

But never again laud the wisdom of Hafiz, for yourselves have seen that he was a confirmed fool.

LXVII

Never, O parrot! speaker of mysteries! let your beak be without sugar. May your head be ever green, and your heart glad, for you displayed a lovely picture of the line of the beloved.

You spoke veiled words to the rivals. For God's sake withdraw the veil from this enigma.

Cast rosewater from the cup on our face, because we are drowned in. sleep, O vigilant fortune!

What a song was this which the musician sang, that the drunk and the sober dance together.

From this opinion which the cupbearer threw into the wine, the revellers will have neither head nor turban.

Although wisdom is the gold of the world, how can it weigh with the love of the lover?

Alexander is not given the water of life. That is not obtained by force or gold.

Come and hear the state of the people of pain, little in word, but much in meaning.

Do not tell the secrets of drunkeness to the sober. Do not ask the story of life from the painting on the wall.

The enemy of our faith is an idol of China, O God! preserve my heart and faith.

He who is kind to his servants, O God! preserve him from calamities.

By the blessings of the banner of the king Mansur, Hafiz became the banner of verse.

LXVIII

Never shall the thought of your cheek be effaced from my distracted mind by the cruelty of the skies or by merciless destiny.

From time without beginning, my heart made covenant with your tresses: to time without end, my promise shall never be broken!

All that my wretched heart contains will depart from my heart, except the sorrow which you have inflicted on me; but that will never leave my heart.

So great is the love of you which has taken hold of my heart and soul, that even if I should lose my life my heart will never lose its love.

If my heart should stray in the chase of beauty, it is pardonable; what can it do? It is suffering, and can never cease from seeking alleviation.

Whosoever does not wish to become maddened like Hafiz, let him never surrender his heart to beauty, nor follow her footsteps.

LXIX

No one has beheld your face, and yet you have a thousand watchers: you are still in the bud, and yet you charm a thousand nightingales.

When I come to your street it seems in no way strange; for many strangers like myself come to your country.

Though I am so far away from you, may no one be far from you. I hope that I may soon delight in your presence.

In love, the cloister and the wine shop are not very far apart; for wheresoever love dwells, a glory radiates from the face of a lover.

The work of the cloister sends forth a splendour where the bell of the devotee rings in the name of the cross.

Where is the lover who has not some loved one to gaze on his state? Where there is pain, there too will be found the healer.

The complaint of Hafiz is not without reason; his tale is strange, and his story wonderful.

LXX

Not everyone who brightens the face knows conquest of hearts. Not everyone who reads books has the knowledge of Alexandria.

Not everyone who sits in high places knows kingship and the laws of sovereignty.

Love has a thousand fetters finer than hair. Not everyone who does not shave his head has the heart of a kalendar.

I am drowned in my tears; what shall I do? not everyone knows how to swim in such an ocean.

The happiness of my sight is from your mole, because I am a jeweller who knows the worth of that pearl.

I lost my heart, and forgot that a child of Adam knows not the love of a Peri.

In form and face my beloved is the queen of the world. Would that she knew how to deal justice.

Fulfilment of promise is the way of the good; not to keep faith is to be tyrannical.

You do not pray, like beggars, in hope of reward; the Lord himself knows how to feed his flock.

With the heart-attracting verse of Hafiz that man will become familiar who possesses a soul for song.

LXXI

Now a breeze of Paradise blows from the garden, and behold me happy with my jug of wine and my beloved.

Why should not the beggar deem himself a monarch today? his canopy the passing cloud, his palace the skirts of the meadow!

The meadow may tell him the tale of Paradise: he is without wisdom who wastes on a future Paradise the money of the present.

Comfort your heart with wine, for the world is a waste, and the end thereof will be that of my clay men will form bricks.

Ask not for faith from an enemy, for it will not yield a ray when you light the candle of the cloister at the lamp of the church.

Write not my name with reproach as a drunkard; for who knows what Fate has written on his brow?

Turn not away your feet from the bier of Hafiz, for though steeped in sin he may yet be welcomed in Heaven.

LXXII

O cupbearer! bring the joy of my youth: bring cup after cup of red wine.

Bring medicine for the disease of love; bring wine, which is the balm of old and young.

Do not grieve for the revolution of time, that it wheeled this way and not that way. Touch the lute in peace.

Wisdom is very wearisome; bring for its neck the noose of wine.

When the rose goes, say, "Go gladly," and drink wine red like the rose.

If the moan of the turtle does not remain, what matter. Bring music in the jug of wine.

The sun is wine and the moon the cup. Pour the sun into the moon.

To drink wine is either good or bad: drink, if it be bad or if it be good.

Her face cannot be seen except in a dream: bring then the medicine of sleep.

Give cup after cup to Hafiz: pour, whether it be sin or sanctity.

LXXIII

O departed from my sight, God guard you! You have slain my soul, but I yet hold you in my heart.

Until such time as the skirt of my shroud trails beneath the foot of my dust, never believe that I will draw back my hand from your garment.

Let me still gaze at the altar of your eyebrows, that at the morning hour I may yet lay the hand of supplication on your neck.

If I should be compelled to go to the Babylonian wizard, I would learn a hundred juggling arts to win you.

Of your mercy grant me access to you, that from this heart-burning I may rain down pearls at your feet.

A hundred rivers have flowed from my eyes into your bosom, in the hope that I might sow the seed of love in your heart.

I weep in the hope that this torrent of tears may water the plant of love in your heart.

The beloved has shed my blood, but I am grateful to her dagger-pointed eye that has freed me from the torture of separation.

One thing I desire before I die, you faithless physician!—that you should ask about this sufferer who longs for you.

O Hafiz! wine and woman and song are not becoming to you. You must abjure them ere I pardon you.

LXXIV

O Heart! how long will you shed my blood unashamed? You, also, O eyes! sleep, and fulfil the desire of the heart.

I am that man, O God, who snatches a kiss from the lips of the beloved. Did you see how the morning prayer was, at last, granted?

How long is the ear of corn to be snatched, like the wind, from the harvest of lovers? Take provision from endeavour, and sow seed yourself.

The bestower of livelihood granted me the desire of this world and of the next; at first the sound of the harp reached my ear, and the tresses touched my hand at last.

The gallery of pictures of China, I know, will not become your palace; however, with the tip of the musky reed I will paint a picture.

O heart! if you do not fly away from sorrow into the kingdom of night, the morning breeze will, at length, bring you tidings from the beloved.

The moon-like idol knelt down and offered wine like ruby. You say, "I have renounced": O Hafiz! be ashamed before the cupbearer.

LXXV

O Hoopoo, I send you eastward to the land of Saba! Behold whence and whither I send you.

It is not just that you should be imprisoned in this pit of pain; therefore I send you forth to the nest of fidelity.

In the road of love there is neither far nor near: I behold you as in my presence, and offer to you my prayers.

Every morning and every evening I send you a caravan of good wishes under the wings of the north and cast winds.

O companion of my heart, removed from my sight, I send you my blessing and my praise.

That the army of sorrow may not devastate your domain, I send you my own valued life to purchase its redemption from plunder.

That the minstrels may tell you of my desire for you, I send you my words and my ghazels, with music and with instruments.

Come hither, O cupbearer, for a heavenly messenger has proclaimed to me these tidings of great joy—"Endure your pain with patience, for I will send you also the remedy."

In your own countenance you may delight in the creation of God, for I have sent you a mirror in which you may gaze on Divinity.

Hafiz, the song of our assembly is a loving memory of you. Hasten! I have sent you a horse and a garment.

LXXVI

O Lord, that smiling rose, which you entrusted to my keeping, I return to your care, to guard her from the envious eye of her garden.

Although she be conveyed a hundred stages from the village of faithfulness, far be the dangers of the magic of the moon from her soul and body!

Wherever she goes, the heart of her friend shall be her companion; the kindness of the well-wisher shall be her shield!

O morning breeze, if you pass by the bounds of Sulima's garden, I demand that you bear a salutation from me to Sulima.

Scatter your musky odour softly over those black tresses, they are the dwelling of dear lovers; do not disturb them.

Say to her, My heart has kept its vow of fidelity to the mole of your cheek; therefore hold sacred those amber-woven tresses.

In that place where they drink to the memory of her beauty, vile would be the reveller who should retain consciousness!

Hope not to find money at the door of the wine tavern. Whoever drinks of this vintage, will cast his wealth into the sea.

Whoever goes in fear of the fever of love is no true lover! Either be her foot upon my head, or be my lip upon her mouth!

The poetry of Hafiz is the beginning of wisdom: praise be to her beauty and her youth.

LXXVII

O musk-scented wind! go to my beloved, touch the knot of her tresses, and bring me life.

Tell her, "O unkind moon! come back, ere your lover die of waiting."

We have given you our heart, and have bought your love for a soul. Do not force the violence of separation on us.

You forgot your servant many a time: keep now your promise to a faithful friend.

O heart! put up with the sorrow of separation and be patient. O eye! do not shed blood any more for this separation.

Since we have no control of the presence of the beloved, do not wash from the eye the thought of the beloved.

O Hafiz! how long will you grieve for the gear of the world. Do not grieve much, for indeed the world is not stable.

LXXVIII

O my heart, ask fair fortune to be your comrade on your journey, and it is enough! a gentle wind from the garden of Shiraz for your herald is enough!

O dervish, wander not again away from the resting place of souls; for you a corner in your monastery is enough!

The atmosphere of the familiar dwelling, and your duty towards your old friend, will excuse you with the travelled wayfarer, well enough!

Scat yourself on the bench in the place of honour, and drink a cup of wine; for this sum of worldly gear and glory is enough!

And if care be hiding in a corner of your heart, the sanctuary of the sacred tavern shall be refuge enough!

Desire not more than suffices you: and bear your burden easily; for a cup of crimson wine, and a woman bright as the moon, are enough.

Heaven delivers unto the hands of the fool the reins of passion: you who esteems yourself wise and virtuous are also foolish enough!

For no other task is there need of you, save the midnight supplications and morning prayers: they are enough!

Accustom not yourself, Hafiz, to count on the gifts of others; for in both worlds the grace of God and the favour of the king are enough!

LXXIX

O my Lord, contrive that my beloved may come back in security, and may deliver me out of the snares of sorrow!

Bring me the dust of the way trodden by my beloved, that I may make my world-beholding eyes her enduring dwelling.

Alas! that on six sides my way is barred by that mole and down, those cheeks and tresses, that form and face.

Today, whilst I am in your power, have compassion on me; tomorrow, when I am clay, of what avail will be your tears of repentance?

O you who use your speech in words and phrases of love, to you we have nothing to say. Go in peace, and good fortune attend you.

Unhappy man, lament not beneath the sword of friends; for that tribe pays the price of blood for those whom they have slain.

God forbid I should reproach you for your heartlessness and oppression; the injustice of the fair is all mercy and kindness.

Hafiz finds it impossible to make a short song about your tresses; the rhyme would stretch out to the day of judgment.

LXXX

On all sides appear signs of inconstancy. No one gives proofs of friendship any longer!

Righteous men reduced to want now hold out to the unworthy the hand of supplication;

And in the changes of the circling spheres the good man gains not a moment's repose from grief;

While fools live in the lap of luxury, for folly is the merchandise which is most esteemed at this time.

And a poet gives out a song as clear as wine, which pours over the heart a flood of joy;

Avarice and greed will not cast him a barleycorn, though he were to sing as tunefully as an angel.

Wisdom whispered yesterday in the car of my mind—
"Go, and in your frailty retain still your endurance!"

"Still make patience your chief purpose; in sickness and grief and want always be patient!"

Come, Hafiz, take this advice to your soul; and if you stagger on your feet, lift up your head and stand upright once more!

LXXXI

One morning a voice called to me from the tavern amicably,—Return, you who have so long attended at this doorway.

Like Jamshid, drink a cup of wine, for a ray from his world-revealing cup may give you a vision of the kingdom of spirits.

At the door of the wine house there are drunken kalenders, who give and take again kingly crowns.

A brick beneath their heads, their feet rest on the seven stars; behold them, and you may see the vanity of power and pomp.

I will lay my head on the dust of the tavern; for though its walls be humble, its roof attains to the stars.

O traveller, be gentle to the beggar at the entrance of the tavern, if you desire to read the mysteries of God.

If they crown you a sultan in the realm of poverty, your least territory will be from the moon to the fishes.

But start not on your journey unless you have Khizar for your comrade; for the road is obscure, and great the peril of missing your way.

O Hafiz, you prey of greed, be ashamed of your ads!—What are they, that you should demand the rewards of both worlds?

You know not how to knock at the door of want; therefore let not slip from your hand the cushion of luxury.

LXXXII

One morning, on the outskirts of his land, thus spoke a wanderer to his neighbour:

"O Sufi, the wine will only run clear after you have kept it fourteen days in the flagon."

Except for the finger of Solomon, what value would his seal-ring boast.

Hundreds of times does God frown on the garb of the devotee, which cloaks a hundred idolatries.

Though shrines be obscure, the anchorite may convey from another world a lamp to illumine them.

Though humanity may be a word without a heart, yet offer you your petition to the benevolent.

The lord of the harvest may reward you, if you are compassionate to the gleaner.

In none do I perceive pleasure or delight, nor medicine for the heart, nor enthusiasm for the faith.

My spirit no longer aspires to Heaven; there is no image of love in the book of my breast.

I have no repose in study or solitude. Where can the learned man find the science of certainty?

Show me the door of the tavern, that may question the seer of my state.

Though the manner of beauty seem disdainful, it may be your destiny, Hafiz, to meet with compassion?

LXXXIII

One kiss from her lip we have not taken, and she is gone: her lovely face we saw not wholly,—and she is gone.

Our converse is changed from gladness to heaviness: we could not hold her back, —and she is gone.

With loving words she would say,—"Never will I depart from the circle of your wishes"; in the end we gained her loving endearments,—and she is gone.

She would say,—"He who desires the joy of my companionship must renounce himself"; we, in the hope of this happiness, renounced ourselves,—and she is gone.

She would walk disdainfully in the meadows of grace, but in the rose garden we plucked not the rosebud of her companionship,—and she is gone.

Each night, like Hafiz, we are given to tears and wailing; for alas! alas! we were never allowed to say farewell,—and she is gone.

LXXXIV

O you, from the splendour of whose face the tulip-bed of life is delightful, come back, because the spring of life is parched without the rose of your face.

If from the eyes tears flow like rain, what wonder? because, without your love, I am alive without life.

I am never apprehensive of the ocean of destruction. On the point of your mouth is the centre of life.

There is an ambush everywhere from the army of accidents; therefore the rider of life runs with loosened reins.

During these moments, when the good fortune of love is possible, understand the lesson of the heart, because the lesson of life is not known.

How long will you enjoy the morning draught and the sweet morning sleep? Awake, take care, because there is no reliance on life.

Yesterday passed away and did not look at us. Last night the beloved passed and she did not look at us.

O Hafiz! speak, because on the page of the world your painting will be long remembered.

LXXXV

O you, who are devoid of knowledge, study till you are a master of knowledge; so long as you are not a wayfarer, how should you be able to point out the way?

In the school of truth, in the presence of the masters of love, work unceasingly, my son, that you may one day become a master!

Sleep and excess have held you back from the exultation of love; wouldst you attain love, you must deny yourself food and slumber.

When the light of the love of God shall descend on your heart and soul, then you will become more glorious than is the sun in the sky.

Wash yourself clean from the dross of the body, that you may find the alchemy of love and be transformed into gold.

From head to foot the light of God will enfold you, when, like the bodiless, you shalt be borne along the path of the glorified.

Plunge for one moment into the sea of God, and think not that the water of the Seven Seas will wet a single feather.

If the countenance of God be the object of your gaze, no doubt can remain that you are among those of clear vision.

Though the bases of your existence shall be upheaved, have no thought in your heart that you are yourself made a ruin.

But if, Hafiz, there be in your mind a wish for wisdom, you will have to become as dust at the door of those endowed with understanding.

LXXXVI

O you who bear the ball of beauty from the beauties of all time, your body is like the straight cypress at the bank of the river.

I swear that the existence of the painting of your mouth is an imaginary point, neither concealed nor known.

We gave our heart to the hand of your eyes, your lips, your tresses: see what this distressed heart suffers at the hand of each of these three.

Let there be a thousand enemies if the friend is with me. I know how to fight, and I am not afraid of the battlefield.

Since your love took its abode in the core of my heart, if I go out from your door I come back by constraint.

If the cypress become vexed before your stature, do not be proud; the sense of tall folk has no fame.

Now, when Hafiz made assurance of your love, his heart fell into captivity like a pawn.

LXXXVII

O wind, whence have you the perfume of my beloved? You have stolen it from her breath!

Beware how you commit a theft on her!—What to you are her waving tresses?

O rose, of what account are you in the sight of her lovely face? Sweet as the musk is she, and you have a thorn.

Sweet-basil, where are you, in competition with the down of her cheek? She is all freshness, and you are defiled with dust.

What are you, narcissus, in the light of her laughing eyes? Hers are only joyous, but your are intoxicated.

O cypress, what are you next to her slender figure? How can you be any longer esteemed in the garden?

O wisdom, what is there to choose between you and the sincerity of her love?

One day, O Hafiz, you will attain to the delight of fulfilment, if you fade not away, meanwhile, in the weariness of waiting.

LXXXVIII

O zephyr, bring fragrance from the dust of the path of the beloved. Take away sorrow from my heart, and bring good tidings of the beloved.

Say a soul-cheering word from the mouth of the beloved. Bring a letter of sweet news from the world of secrets.

In order that I may perfume my nostrils with your sweet gale, bring a little fragrance from the breath of the beloved.

I conjure you by your fidelity, bring dust of the path of that dearly beloved without the dust which appears from strangers.

It is a long time since the heart beheld the face of the beloved. O cupbearer, bring that mirror-like cup.

Bring some dust from the path of the beloved for the blindness of the enemy, for the healing of this blood-shedding eye.

The mad heart does not come back by chain. Bring a noose from the curling lock of the beloved.

Inexperience and simplicity of heart are not the way of the venturesome. Bring news from that sorceress sweetheart.

O bird of the garden, thanks for this, that you are in joy. Bring news of the rosegarden to captives of the cage.

The desire of the soul became bitter from patience which lacked the beloved. Bring a kiss from that sweet sugar-shedding lips.

What is the tattered robe of Hafiz worth? Colour it with wine, and then bring him drunk and ruined to the highway of the market.

LXXXIX

O zephyr, ring perfume from the street of such an one. I am weak and sick of grief; bring me the ease of the soul.

Pour elixir of desire on our fruitless heart; bring me a trace of the dust of the door of the beloved.

In the ambush of vision I quarrel with my own heart; bring me arrow and bow made from her eyebrow and glance.

I am become old in indigence, separation, and grief of heart: bring me a cup of wine from the hand of youth.

Give to the deniers also two or three cups of this wine, and if they do not take it bring it swiftly to me.

O cupbearer! do not put off till tomorrow the pleasure of today, or bring me assurance of tomorrow's safety from the book of Fate.

Last night my heart went forth from the screen when Hafiz said, "O zephyr, bring me perfume from the street of such an one."

XC

O zephyr, do not withhold passing by the house of the beloved, and not withhold news from her from the poor lover.

In thanks for this, that you blossomed according to the desire of the heart: oh rose! do not withhold breeze of union from the bird of the morning.

All our hopes depend upon one glance do not withhold this from old friends.

I was the companion of your banquet when you were like the new moon; now that you are the full moon, do not withhold your glance.

The world, and everything that is in it, are mean and insignificant: do not withhold this pittance from the people possessed; of divine knowledge.

The poet conveys your favours to the end of the world: do not withhold from him allowance and provision for the journey.

When you seek praise of your virtues, in return for that praise do not withhold silver and gold.

Now that your crimson lip is the spring of the water of Life, speak, and do not withhold sugar from the parrot.

The dust of sorrow will blow off, and your condition will be better, O Hafiz Therefore do not withhold your water of your eye.

XCI

She said: You went forth to behold the new moon; be ashamed of the moon of your eyebrow, and depart!

Through life your heart has been the slave of my tresses; be not so unmindful of remaining at the side of your friends.

Sell not the scent of your intelligence for the tresses of the beloved; for in that a thousand musk-pods can be obtained for half a barleycorn.

In this old cornfield expel not that the seed of love and loyalty will leap to the eye until the season of harvest.

Cuphearer, bring me wine, and I will read you the riddle, the wizardry of the old stars and the wanderings of the new moon.

The disc of the waning moon at the close of each month shows you a sign of what has been the fate of the crowns of kings.

O Hafiz! the doorway of the keeper of the tavern is the place where you may listen to and read the tale of love.

XCII

She who has stolen my heart has departed, giving no warning to her lover, remembering not the comrade of the journey.

Either fate misguided me in the path of friendship, or it was she who journeyed not by the king's highway.

Whilst I stood there, like the taper, and offered my life for hers, she came not, like the morning wind, to solace me on my way.

I said: Perhaps I may soften her heart by my tears; but no raindrop left an impression on that marble heart.

And though in my despair I tore off my plumes and broke my wings, even this would not expel from my heart this tameless passion of love.

Everyone who gazed upon your face kissed my eyes, for that which my eyes did was not done without wisdom.

The tongue, the reed of Hafiz will never reveal your secret to the crowd as long as your lover loses not his head.

XCIII

Show your face, and make me forget my existence: tell the wind, "Take away all the harvest of the burnt."

We, who gave heart and eye to the storm of misery, bid the flood of sorrow come and shake the house from its foundation.

Who can smell her tressess, like pure ambergris? Alas! O foolish heart! forget this word.

Tell the heart, "Put out the flame of the fire-temple of Persia." Tell the eye, "Put to shame the face of the Tigris of Baghdad."

Without making an effort you will not reach your goal in this path: if you want reward, obey the master.

Last night she said, "I will kill you with my long eyelashes." O God! take away from her mind the thought of cruelty.

Promise to see me for a moment on the day of my death, and then take me happy and free to the grave.

May the good fortune of the mage last for ever, because the rest is easy; let everyone else go away and forget me.

Henceforth my pale face dwells in the dust of the door of the beloved. Bring wine, and blot sorrow at once from my memory.

O Hafiz! think of the tenderness of the beloved's heart. Go and take away this cry and complaint from her court.

XCIV

Show your face and say to me, "Sacrifice your life for me." Say, "Kindle with your soul the fire of the butterfly before the candle."

Look at my thirsty lip, and do not withhold water. Come to him who is killed by you, and raise him from the dust.

Play on the harp and be content; and if there be no aloe wood, what fear? Consider my love fire, my heart aloe wood, and my body a censer.

Come to delight and singing; doff the religious habit and dance; otherwise sit in the corner and wear the habit of hypocrisy.

Let the friend be my helper, and the two worlds my enemy. Let fortune fail me, and the surface of the earth take up arms against me.

Do not abandon the dervish if he does not possess silver and gold; consider his tears as silver, and account his face as gold.

Do not take thought of going, O beloved! be with us for a moment. Seek delight at the bank of the river, and take the cup into your hand.

Consider this fire of my heart and water of my eye as gone from me: consider my pale colour, my dry lip, and my wet bosom.

Take off the cowl from the head and drink pure wine: spend silver, and go and embrace the beloved with silver bosom.

Hafiz! adorn the banquet, and tell the admonisher, "See my assembly and give up the pulpit."

XCV

Spring has returned once more, with the rapturous rose: in the rapture of gazing on the cheek of the rose uproot the plant of sorrow from your heart.

The soft west wind has come; the rose in its passion has rent its glorious garment.

Learn, my heart, the way of truth from the transparent water; in righteousness strive to be free from the cypress of the meadow.

The bride of the rose, with her jewels and smiles, has robbed me of my heart and my faith.

The passion of the nightingale, and the song of the bird of love, have come to rejoice at the coming forth of the rose from her house of mourning.

Behold how the breeze has, with his hand, entangled the tresses of the rose; look how the locks of the hyacinth bend over the face of the jessamine!

Learn the story of the wheeling sphere from the cup, Hafiz! as the voice of the singer and the wisdom of the wise counsel you.

XCVI

The beloved who made my house the home of an angel; who from head to foot was like an angel, free from faults;

That moon who was the joy of my heart, who was graced with beauty, urbanity, fascination, and intelligence;

Of whom my heart said, "I will abide in her city," but knew not, most miserable, that the beloved was a wanderer.

That friend has a relentless star torn from my arms! What shall I do? The moon in its course has caused me this disaster.

Nor has the veil fallen from the secret of my heart only, for, by the will of Heaven, every veil of enchantment has been rent asunder.

Sweet is the rose, and sweet the green border of the stream; alas, that this pleasure should be so fleet!

Sweet were the moments I spent with my beloved. What time still remains to me must be passed ignorantly and unavailingly.

The nightingale slew himself through jealousy, because the rose wooed the wind in the hour of dawn.

Excuse him, O my heart, for you are poor, and she was crowned queen of the kingdom of beauty.

Every gift of happiness which God has bestowed on Hafiz has been the reward of the nightly prayer and the morning supplication.

XCVII

The bird of my heart is a sacred bird, whose nest is the throne of God; tired of its cage of the body, it is weary of the way of the world.

If once the bird of the soul flies from this pit, it finds its resting place again only at the gate of that palace.

And when the bird of my heart soars upward, its place is the tallest tree; for know that our falcon finds rest only on the top of the throne.

The shadow of fair fortune is cast upon the world wherever our bird spreads its vans over the world.

In both worlds its home is only in the highest sphere; its body is from the pit, but its soul is limited to no place.

Only the highest heaven is the bower of our bird; its pleasance is in the rose garden of Paradise.

O Hafiz, you troubled one, when you utter a word about unity, write unity with your reed on the page of man and angel.

XCVIII

The breath of the breeze is shedding musk; the old world has renewed its youth!

The tulip is offering its cup to the jessamine; the eye of the narcissus glances towards the anemone.

The pain of parting from the nightingale spreads lamentation to the pavilion of the rose.

Blame me not if I leave the temple to seek the tavern: the sermon to the assembly was long, and time was slipping away.

Heart, my heart, if you cast away until tomorrow the pleasures of today, who will be your surety for the money of life which still remains to you?

This month of carnival let not the cup be set down out of your hand, for this sun will disappear from sight until the close of the fast of Ramazan.

The rose is priceless! Count its presence as a gift; for it enters the garden this way and departs that way.

Singer, this is an assembly of friends; read your rhyme and sing your song. How long will you repeat, "As it has been so will it ever be"?

Hafiz for your sake entered the house of life; prepare to bid him farewell, for he will soon be going!

XCIX

The coin of the Sufi is not altogether without alloy: many religious habits deserve to be burnt in the fire.

Our Sufi, who is proud of his morning prayer, look at him at evening time when he makes merry.

It will be good to bring the touchstone in our midst, so that he may be covered with shame in whom there is alloy.

He who is brought up in softness and ease cannot travel to the beloved. To make love is the joy of the adventurous.

If the down on the cheeks of the cupbearer charm in this way, many faces will be painted with tears.

How long will you grieve for the base world? Drink wine, and trouble not the heart of the wise.

Let the wineseller take away the religious habit and the prayer carpet of Hafiz, if the wine be poured from the hand of that moon-like cupbearer.

C

The desire for the wind of spring took me towards the desert. The wind brought your perfume and took away rest from me.

Wherever there was a heart your eye lured it away from the path; it did not take away only my sick, my broken heart.

Last night the cup of wine, on reaching your lip, claimed to bestow life; it derived this honour from your life-giving and soul-bestowing lip.

Last night the chain of your love tied the hand of my desire: the army of sorrow threw down the power of the army of my wisdom.

The glance of that girl of arched eyebrow robbed us on the highway: the mole on the cheek of that slender cypress deprived us of our hearts.

My tears brought to the path your stony heart. The flood can carry a stone to the bank of the river.

Do not talk of the sweet song of the nightingale before Hafiz: no mention can be made of the nightingale before the parrot.

CI

The east wind at the dawn of day brought a perfume from the tresses of my beloved, which immediately cast my foolish heart into fresh agitation.

I imagined that I had uprooted that flower from the garden of my heart, for every blossom which sprang up from its suffering bore only the fruits of pain.

From fear of the attacks of her love I set my heart free with bloody strife: my heart dropped gouts of blood which marked my footsteps.

I beheld from her terrace how the glory of the moon veiled itself in confusion before the face of that dazzling sun.

At the voice of the singer and the cupbearer I go to the door in and out of season; for the messenger comes with trouble from a weary road.

Any gift of my beloved I take as courteous and kind, whether it be Mohammedan, Christian, or Jewish.

Heaven protect her eyebrows from harm; for though they brought me to despair, yet with a gracious greeting they have given consolation to the sick heart.

Joy to the time and the hour when I freed myself from the snare of her braided tresses, and gained a victory which even my foe admitted.

From envy of the tresses of my beloved the breeze lavished all the musk which she had carried from Tartary.

I was amazed when I discovered last night cup and jug beside Hafiz; but I said no word, for he used them in Sufi manner.

CII

The fast is ended, the Feast has arrived, and hearts are exalted, and the wine runs in the tavern, the red wine we long to drink!

The hour of the abstainer is over, the hour of enjoyment has come and of joyous drinkers!

Why should condemnation be heaped upon him who, like me, drinks wine? this is neither crime nor failing in the happy lover!

The drinker of wine in whom is neither deceit nor insincerity, is better than he who deals in deceptions.

We are neither hypocritical revellers, nor the companions of the deceitful; He to whom no secrets are hidden is aware of this.

We discharge all our duties, and do wrong to no man; and whatever we are told is unlawful, we say not that it is lawful.

Of what importance is it that you and I should drain a few cups of wine? wine is the blood of the vine; it is not the blood of men!

This is not a sin which throws all into confusion; and were it a sin, where is the man who is guiltlesss of sins?

Hafiz, abandon the How and the Wherefore, and for this passing moment drink your wine. His wisdom has concealed from us the meaning of the words How and Why.

CIII

The heart is a screen behind which He hides His love: His eye is the glass which reflects His face.

I, who would not bend my head to both worlds, yield my neck to the yoke of His mercies.

You enjoy the tree of Paradise, I the memory of my beloved; thus each man's thoughts are shaped to the measure of his inclinations.

What should I do within that holy place, wherein the wind is the screen of the shrine of His sanity

If I have soiled my garment, what harm can I do? the universe is the witness of His purity.

Majnun is long departed, now comes our turn: to each one is given five days' sojourn.

The kingdom of love, and the wealth of enjoyment, all are given by the hand of His destination.

If we have offered our hearts as a ransom, what should we fear? The goal at which we aim is the glory of His salvation.

Cease not to regard His image as the idol of your eye, for its cell is the shrine of His privacy.

Every rose which paints the meadow is a sign of the beauty and odour of His beneficence.

Regard not my poverty, for the heart of Hafiz is a treasury of His benevolence.

CIV

The glad tidings have come, the spring is returned in its splendour: if the gift is bestowed, expend it on wine and roses

The song of the bird is heard once more, but where is the wine flagon? The nightingale is complaining—"Who will withdraw the veil from the rose?"

I will fling my rags into the fire, rose red with wine, for the wine keeper will not give for them the lees of his cask.

From the cheek of a cupbearer, radiant as the moon, gather a rose; for around the edge of the garden the violet dawns.

In the land of love set not a foot without one to lead you, for he is lost who walks this road without a guide.

What can he know of the fruits of Paradise, who has never kissed the apple of a beauty's cheek?

The smiles of the cupbearer have stolen my heart from my hand. I can no longer talk or listen to any other.

The marvels on the way of love, my comrade, are many; in that desert the lion fears the fawn.

My heavenly guide, help me on this sacred journey, for to the wilderness of love no end is visible!

Hafiz has not gathered a rose in this field of beauty; perchance the wind of humanity has not blown over this garden.

The spring has passed away: find out the righteous man; for time is flying, and Hafiz has not yet drunk the wine.

CV

The joyful news has come that the days of sorrow are not without end; those did not stay, nor will these last for ever.

What though I was even as nothing in the sight of my loved one, my rival will not be honoured for ever.

The keeper of the gate will smite with his sword, and no one will dwell in the heart of the harem for ever.

Count as gain, my candle, the love of the moth, for before dawn this desire will cease for ever.

An angel from Heaven has brought me a message: "No one on earth will remain unhappy for ever."

What space is there for joy or grief in the web of good and evil, since no sign on the page of life will remain for ever.

It is told that this was the song in the house of Jamshid: "Jamshid himself will not endure for ever."

O rich man, be swift to help the poor man, for your gold and your silver will not be your for ever.

On the vault of heaven is inscribed in starfire: "Nothing, save the righteous of the righteous man, will remain for ever.

The morning brought me the consoling message, that none will remain the slave of misfortune for ever.

O Hafiz, never abandon your benevolence, for evil and oppression will not be seen for ever.

CVI

The picture of your face is with me in all my ways: the perfume of your hair is wrapped around my living soul.

I am revolted by the fool who would prohibit love; the fairness of your face is an all-sufficing answer.

Behold at least what says the apple of your chin,—"A thousand Egyptian Josephs have fallen into my well."

If my hand fails to reach your long tresses, it is the fault of my short arm and my unhappy destiny.

Say to the watcher who keeps guard in the palace of kings, "There is one who sits in the dust in a corner of my court

"Whose picture, although veiled from sight, is ever present to the contemplation of my mind.

"If Hafiz comes a suppliant to my door, open it to him, for through long years he has been longing to look upon his moon."

CVII

The love you have known will cause you happiness, for in this manner does Fate administer your affairs.

The purpose of Time in thus proving you is to set on your heart the seal of self-denial and virtue.

And for this cause the sacred volume is exalted, because time has examined it.

The man who is valiant in wisdom is he who in all matters considers first the path he should follow.

The palate of his soul will be saved from the bitterness of sorrow who receives into his mouth the sugar of gratitude!

He will eat of the fruit of Life who considers well the way he should follow.

When he sees no cause for strife, he will clasp the cup; and when he sees the time for fighting, he will seize the sword.

In the time of trouble avert not your face from hope, for the soft marrow abides in the hard bone.

Sugar finds after abstinence the perfection of sweetness, and for this cause it first dwells in a narrow channel.

However arrogantly your adversary may bear himself, congratulate yourself that his very arrogance will hold his hand.

Although he has uttered false words about this house of fortune, retribution will come through his wife and child and kindred.

May the years of your life, be lasting for this fortune is a blessing vouchsafed to the deeds of men and angels.

Hafiz, you are a monarch in the kingdom of speech; every moment you achieve victories in the plain of words.

CVIII

The nightingale, from the branch of the cypress, sang this lesson last night in divine Pehlevi to the listeners:

Come, for the rose tree is on fire with the fire of Moses, that you may learn from the bush the subtlety of unity.

The birds of the garden are singing and jesting, that the master may drink his wine to the old Pehlevi songs.

Blessed to the beggar is the hour when he sleeps on his carpet; for such enjoyment is not permitted beneath the crown of kings.

Jamshid took nothing from out the world save the cup; take heed that you attach not your heart to the gear of the world!

Well said the aged peasant to his son, "O light of my eyes, save what you have sown nothing will you reap!"

Perhaps the cuphearer has bestowed on Hafiz more than his share, for the tassel of his turban is disordered.

CIX

The phoenix of the summit of fair fortune will fall into our snare if you happen to pass by our dwelling.

I will throw up my cap in delight, like a bubble of water, if a reflection of your face fall into our cup.

When the wind has no access to your court, how can there fall a chance for our salutation?

When my soul was consecrated to your lip, I thought a drop of pure water would fall upon our palate.

I thought your ringlet said, "Do not make life the means, because abundance of such prey falls into our snare.

Since kings have not the right to kiss the dust of this door, when will there be the favour of a return to our salutation?

Do not go from this door in disappointment; try your chance; perhaps the die of fortune will fall to your name.

At the night in which the moon of hope rises from the horizon, would that the reflection of that light might fall on our terrace!

Whenever Hafiz speaks of the dust of your street, the breeze of the rose garden of life falls into our nostrils.

CX

The patient nightingale once more from the straight cypress sang, "Far be the evil eye from the face of the rose!"

O rose! in thanks for this, that you blossomed according to the desire of my heart, do not be haughty towards nightingales sick of love.

If the devotee is hopeful for the houris of Paradise and for palaces, to us taverns are as palaces, and the beloved a houri of Paradise.

I do not complain against the hand of your absence. So long as there is no absence, presence does not give pleasure.

If others are glad and joyous in pleasure and delight, love for the beloved is the source of delight to us.

Drink wine to the sound of the harp, and do not be sorry; and if anyone tell you, "Do not drink wine," say, "God is forgiving."

O Hafiz! why do you complain of the grief of separation? After separation there is union, and after darkness there is light.

CXI

The profit of this workshop of ours is all vanity. Set wine before me, for the gear of this world is all vanity.

With heart and soul we desire the companionship of the beloved, and perchance heart and soul are all vanity.

That which comes to our bosom without heart-heaviness is true joy; and since they are attained by labour and trouble, but the gardens of Paradise are vanity.

Be not grateful to the shade tree for shade; for if you, moving cypress, but gaze upon us kindly, they are all vanity.

The five days you are allowed to linger in this caravanserai, rest in peace, for time itself is but vanity.

O cupbearer, we are waiting on the shore of this ocean of mortality; grasp the cup, for, in the distance from lip to mouth, all is vanity!

Waste not a thought on its withering, but be joyous like the rose; for the pomp of the passing world is all vanity.

O devout man, feel not safe from the deceptions of pride; for the difference between the cloister and the temple of the infidel is but vanity.

What have not I, sorrow-stricken man, endured from evil destiny; but confession and complaint are both alike a vanity.

The name of Hafiz has gained a good report; but in the fellowship of those who haunt the tavern good report and evil report are both vanity.

CXII

The road of love is a road without end, and in which there is no help save to abandon our souls.

Seek not to alarm us with the prohibitions of reason, for that watchman has no authority in our land.

You who give up your heart to love, you have happy moments! When a thing is good, what need of wishing for something better?

Demand of your own eye, who wishes to lure you? O, my soul, it is not the fault of fortune, nor the sin of the stars.

To him who has a far-seeing eye, it is possible to discover the first silver of the new moon: it is not given to every eye to discern that crescent.

Count it as gain to tread the path of intoxication, for it, like that which leads to a treasure, is not visible to everyone.

The weeping of Hafiz makes no impression on you: I am pained to find your heart not less hard than stone.

CXIII

The rose would not be fair without the face of my beloved: the spring would not be brave without the blood of the vine.

The outskirts of the lawn and the winds of the garden would not be gracious without the tulip-cheek of the beloved.

The honey mouth and radiant image of the beloved would not be perfect without her kiss and her caress.

The movement of the cypress and the madness of the rose would not be exquisite without the song of the nightingale.

No picture traced by the touch of genius would be as lovely as the image of my idol.

Glorious are the garden, the rose, and wine, but they would not be so wanting the presence of my beloved.

Your life, Hafiz, is but debased money; it is not sufficiently valuable to cast among the throng at a festival.

CXIV

The violet is vexed with envy of your musk-scented tresses; at your heart-rejoicing smile the rosebud rends its leaves.

O my perfume-exhaling rose, consume not your own nightingale, who with heartfelt sincerity prays for you night after night!

Behold the might of Love! how, in his pomp and splendour, he dared, beggar though he be, to break off a fragment of the crown of royalty.

I, whom the breath of angels made sad, can for your sake endure the quarrels of the world.

To love you is the destiny inscribed on my forehead; the dust of your threshold is my Paradise, your radiant cheek my nature, to pleasure you my repose.

The rags of the saint, and the goblet of wine, although they do not harmonize well, I have blended into one, because of you.

Love, like the beggar, still conceals treasure in his sleeve; and soon he who was your suppliant will be exalted to sovereignty.

The resting place of your form is my throne and altar: O my queen, do not abandon your place.

This bewilderment of wine, and this delirium of love, will not depart from my head until I abase it, full of desire, in the dust at the door of your dwelling.

Your cheek is like a fair meadow, especially when, in the lovely spring, Hafiz, sweet of speech, is your nightingale.

CXV

The zephyr at the feast of the rose bestows wine to the soul again. Where is the sweet nightingale? tell it to sing a song.

Oh heart! do not complain of separation, inasmuch as in the world there are sorrow and pleasure, thorn and rose, and degradation and exaltation.

I am bent like the bow from sorrow, and yet I do not give up the arched eyebrows which are darting arrows.

Do not relate to enemies the story of the night of separation, because the breast of the revengeful is not a warder of secrets.

The distress of my heart is revealed by your locks; yes, it is not strange if the musk be a tale-teller.

A thousand eyes are looking at your face, and you are not looking at the face of any one, through grace.

O heart! if you are burnt, do not complain of the burning; continue to breathe his love, and bear with pain.

The dust of our heart will make the eyes of the enemy blind. O Hafiz! put your face in the dust and say your prayers.

CXVI

His messenger, who has arrived from the country of my Friend, has brought from the secret letter of my Friend an amulet for my life.

He gives me a token of the greatness of my Friend; he tells me a story of the glory of my Friend.

I have given him my heart for his glad tidings, but I feel shame for my poor counters, which I scatter on the way of my Friend.

Praise be to God! that, with the help of propitious fate, I have brought all my desires into accord with the desires of my Friend.

Why should I command the movements of the spheres, and the changes of the moon, since all their revolvings are the choice of my Friend?

Prepare me, O wind of the morning, an unguent made of that fortune-favoured earth which lay in the pathway of my Friend.

We will remain at the threshold of our Friend, our heads bent to the earth in prayer, nor raise ourselves till we fall asleep on the bosom of the Friend.

If an enemy should draw a breath to injure Hafiz, why should I fear? since, glory be to God, I have no cause to be ashamed of my Friend.

CXVII

You gaze upon me, and each moment you increase my pain: I gaze on you, and each moment my love becomes greater.

You inquire not about my state; I know not what are your hidden thoughts: you make ready for me no medicine; mayhap you know not that I am ill.

This is not right, that you should fling me to earth and then pass me by! Ah, return, and ask once more, how it is with me; for I would be to you even as the dust of your path!

I will not remove my hand from your garment even if I am turned to clay; for when you pass by my grave, my hand shall catch hold of your raiment.

The pains of your love have deprived me of words; restore it to me again! How long will you take away my breath, not say to me, "Take it back!"

One night in the darkness I demanded my heart again from your tresses. I beheld your cheek, and drank the cup of your mouth.

I drew you quickly to my breast, and your tresses blazed in flame; I pressed lip to lip, and gave for your ransom my soul and heart.

When without me you wander for your enjoyment through the meadows, a sallow tear starts and falls down my cheek.

Be gracious to Hafiz! say to my enemy, Give up your life! If I can win warmth from you, what can trouble me in the chill breath of my enemy!

CXVIII

Those preachers who in the pulpit and at the altar show so much ostentation, when they go into their chamber act very differently.

My soul is amazed at the brazen-faced preachers, who practise so little of all they preach in the pulpit.

I had a doubt, and inquired of the wise ones of the assembly—"Wherefore do those who order penance seldom praise penance themselves?"

Surely those talkers who are so haughty and insincere in the work of their judge, have no belief in a day of judgment!

O Lord, mount this band of braggarts on the backs of asses, for all this pride they have taken from their slaves and mules.

Bow yourself down in adoration, O angel, at the door of the tavern of love, for therein is kneaded the clay from which mankind has been moulded.

When surpassing beauty has annihilated a world of lovers, a fresh world springs up to love from the Invisible.

I am the slave of the keeper of the tavern, whose beggars in their independence fling dust on the head of riches.

Spring up, beggar of the monastery! for in the temple of the Magi they pour a water that perfects all hearts.

Empty your house of idols, that it may be converted into a shrine of love! for those who lust hold idols in their hearts and souls.

In the dawn there is a tumult around God's throne, and Wisdom calls aloud, "It is the Angelic Choir which chants the verses of Hafiz."

CXIX

Through your black eyelashes you have made a thousand breaches in my faith: come, that from your alluring eye I may pluck a thousand pains.

O comrade of my heart, from whom all remembrance of your friends has passed away, may no day ever come in which I sit for a moment without thought of you!

The world which withers and the world which abides I will offer as a ransom for my loved one and the cupbearer; for I deem the sovereignty of the world the lowly companion of love.

If the beloved prefer a stranger in my stead, let the beloved be the judge; but let it never be lawful for me to prefer life before the beloved.

From the heat of the flame of separation I have been drowned like a rose in dew; waft me, O night wind, a breeze from the beloved.

The tale of the longing which this verse portrays is sure beyond doubt, for Hafiz himself has dictated it to me.

CXX

Your beauty, like my love, has attained perfection! I joy that neither the one nor the other has suffered decrease.

To my imagination it does not appear, that in the visions of wisdom any form of loveliness should excel this!

Every moment that I am with you a year seems to me like a day, and every moment I am without you the twinkling of an eye is as a year.

Every hour of life were delight, if spent with you: were life only one day, that day would be my heart's desire.

How may I behold, O beloved, the image of your face in my dreams, when out of my dreams I have never yet beheld anything save an image.

Have compassion on my unhappy heart, for the love of your fair face has withered me, like a waning moon.

O Hafiz, make no complaint if you seek to win your beloved; for you will yet have to endure the greater load of separation.

CXXI

O gaze awhile in tranquillity of heart on the fair face of your moon, is better than to wear the crown of kings through a whole life of honour.

By Heaven, I am envious of my own eye on that cheek, that the look of such a lovely countenance should be so disdainful.

My heart has gone, and I know not what is become of my beloved; for my life has departed, and no tidings come to me from any quarter.

My breath has come to an end, and my eye is still unsatiated; beyond this there is left to me neither longing nor wish.

Ruffle not, O breeze, one tress of that Peri, for Hafiz would give a thousand lives to purchase the thread of one single hair!

CXXII

We are not come to this door in pursuit of riches or glory; we are come for a shelter from evil chances.

Travellers in the stages of the journey of love, we are come a long way from the realm of non-existence to attain the climes of life.

We beheld the fresh down on your cheek, and we come from the garden of Paradise seeking the grass of love.

With such treasures whose treasurer is the faithful spirit, we arrive as beggars at the gate of the king's house.

O vessel of grace, where is your anchor of patience? for in the ocean of clemency we are overwhelmed by our iniquities!

Our honour is departing! O cloud, blot out our sins, for black are the characters of our names in the book of deeds.

Hafiz, cast aside your woolly garment of hypocrisy, for we follow the path of the caravan with the fire of our sighs.

CXXIII

Were God to chastise every one for his offences, the earth would be full of lamentations, and time full of wailings.

In the sight of the Lord mountains are as grass; at one time He pardons a mountain, and at another He condemns a grass blade.

Your sins are as immense as the surface of the earth: do you not know that it is your iniquity which eclipses the moon in the sky.

You are apparelled in pure raiment, O heart! but your iniquities will be made known tomorrow, when the accuser shall demand justice upon you.

The whole night long, in shame for my sins, I will weep so unceasingly that the place of my prayer shall that night be grown with grass.

The night of my leave taking rivers of tears shall flow from my eyes, so that my beloved shall find those rivers in every land.

When the king, O Hafiz, has decreed that a man must die, who will have the courage or power to go before the king and oppose him?

CXXIV

We will speak no evil, neither incline towards injustice: we will blacken no man's countenance, nor stain our own raiment.

We will not harp much or little on the shortcomings of rich or poor; it is wise that we commit no manner of evil deed.

We will journey through the world peaceably in the sight of all wayfarers, nor waste a thought on black steed or gold saddle.

We will not write a line of lies on the Book of Wisdom: we will not mix with the mysteries of Truth the pages of magic.

If the austere man deny us wine, we will not do him homage with pure and refined wine.

And if the king will not drink with dignity the draught of the revellers, we will in no way offer it to him in its truth and its clearness.

Heaven hurls in shipwreck the vessel of the wise; therefore it were wiser not to rock ourselves on that heavy sea.

If the envious speak evil of you, and the friend be wroth, say to him—"Be calm, we lend no ear to the fool!"

Hafiz, if an enemy has spoken lies of your backslidings, pay no heed! If he speak truth, let us not strive with the speech of truth!

CXXV

What am I that I should disdain that fragrant mind; you do confer favours on me whose forehead desires the dust of your doorway for a crown!

Tell me, you capturer of hearts, who has taught you this kindness; for I will never impute this idea to those who watch you.

O holy bird, be my guide on the path of my wishes, for the journey I undertake is a long journey, and I am new to journeying!

O morning breeze, carry with you my service and say—"Do not forget me at the hour of morning prayer!"

Happy the day when I shall bind up my chattels for the journey and when the companions shall ask of me from the head of your village.

Show me the path to your secret retreat that I may drink wine with you, and free myself from worldly grief.

Lofty and world-enthralling is the dignity of verse! therefore command the lord of the sea that he may fill your mouth with pearls.

O Hafiz, it is well that in your pursuit of the jewel of union your eye may make an ocean of tears and yourself be swallowed up in it.

CXXVI

What has induced this intoxication I know not! Who was the cupbearer? from whence came the wine?

What manner of song has the master of music given forth, that he has woven into his singing the voice of the beloved?

The breeze, with its sweet story, is like the hoopoo of Solomon, which brought tidings of joy from the rose gardens of Sheba.

You also bring wine to the cup and take the path of the meadows, for the bird song has returned with sweet melodies.

Welcome and joyful greeting to the coming of the rose and the wild rose: the joy-dispensing violet has cone, and the lily has brought its purity.

Heart my heart, lament not that, even as the rosebud, you are enclosed within your own deeds, for the morning breeze brings soft winds to unloose all bonds.

The smile of the cupbearer has brought healing to my stricken heart; lift up your head, the physician has arrived with the remedy!

If I am a disciple of the ancient Mage; be not wroth with me, O shaikh! for you only gave me a promise, and he has brought me the substance.

Fate appears now inclined to serve Hafiz as a slave, since, fleeing for safety, it has led me to the door of your fortune.

CXXVII

Wherefore should I not persevere in following the path to my own land? Why should I not wish to be as the earth in the village of my beloved?

No longer able to bear the grief of estrangement and care, I will return to my own city and become my own king.

I will be one of those who are admitted behind the veil of the union; I will become one of the slaves of my beloved.

Since the events of life are concealed from our sight, would that on the Day of Destiny I might be discovered in the company of the loved one.

Perpetually have my pleasures been love and revelry; henceforward I will labour and devote myself to my own work.

Hitherto I have been led by the hand of Destiny to be a dreamer and an idler; I will strive henceforward to be the worker of my own work.

Perchance, O Hafiz, the compassion of eternity, without beginning, may be your guide; if not to eternity, everlasting will be your confusion.

CXXVIII

Who can relate the state of bloody hearts? Who seeks revenge for the death of Jamshid from the sky?

Except the sage, sitting by the wine cask, who can relate to us the secret of wisdom?

If the drunken narcissus grow again, may it be ashamed before the eye of the worshippers of wine!

He who, like the tulip, became a drinker, will wash his face with blood because of this tyranny.

As the harp spoke much which was miserable, cut its chord, that it may not cry again.

My heart will open like the rosebud, if it smell the tulip-coloured cup.

If Hafiz can, he will carry his head to the sacred temple of the winejar.

CXXIX

Whosoever became the confidant of his heart remained in the fold of the beloved, and he who did not know this matter remained ignorant.

If my heart is distracted do not find fault with me. Thanks be to God that my heart did not remain behind the screen of conceit.

The Sufis took back all their apparel which was pledged for wine. It was our religious habit which remained in the house of the wine seller.

Religious mendicants all passed away drunk, and their story is forgotten. Ours is the tale which has remained at the head of every market.

I had a religious habit, and it used to hide a hundred defects; it was pledged for wine and musicians, and the defeats remained.

Than the echo of the talk of love, I did not hear anything more pleasant. Its great remembrance remained in this round dome.

Every ruby-coloured wine of which I took a crystal cup became the water of regret, and in my eye remained the jewel of tears.

Save my heart, which from time without beginning, till time without end, is enamoured of you, I did not hear of any one who remained for ever your lover.

The narcissus became sick in the effort to become like your eye. It did not acquire its magic, and remained sick.

The picture lover was so much astonished at your beauty, that his tale remained everywhere, on the gate and on the wall.

The heart of Hafiz went one day to the theatre of your tresses meaning to return, but it remained ever ensnared.

CXXX

Whosoever has thought with love of the down on your cheeks shall not step out of your circle for his life.

On the day of resurrection, when I shall lift up my head from the dust of the grave, the scar of my madness after you shall be in the very core of my heart.

May the long shelter of your curling locks be on my head, because in this shelter is the only rest of my heart, which is mad in love.

Come forth from the screen for a moment, heart my heart, because hereafter there may be no union.

How long will you permit, O perfect pearl, that the pupil of my eye should be an ocean of sorrow?

From the tip of my very eyelash water is flowing; come, if you have the inclination, to see the flow of the river.

Yes, your eye, and its amorous glances, is not inclined to Hafiz. Pride is the quality of the cruel narcissus.

CXXXI

Whosoever keeps the cause of the people of fidelity, God preserves him, in all circumstances, from misfortune.

If you have the desire that the beloved may not break off the covenant, hold the cord, so that she may preserve the covenant with you.

I will not tell the story of the friend except in the presence of the friend, because the friend preserves the speech of the friend.

My head, heart, and soul are sacrificed for that beloved who observes the right of society, of kindness, and fidelity.

Live in such a way, O heart! that in case your foot slip, the angel, with the two hands of blessing, may preserve you.

She did not preserve my heart, but she said: What arises from the hand of the slave God will preserve. O zephyr! if you see my heart in those tresses, kindly tell it how it may preserve its place.

Where is the dust of your path, that Hafiz may preserve it in memory of the perfume of the wind!

CXXXII

Whosoever leaves your street in shame, his acts will never prosper; and he himself will in the end depart in shame.

The traveller who is seeking the road to the beloved will want the light of guidance; for if he choose the wrong road he will never attain his aim.

Take a pledge for the remainder of life from wine, and from the beloved: alas! for the time which is wholly wasted in idleness.

O guide of my abandoned heart, let me entreat God for help, for the stranger on the path wants a guide.

The seal of Fate is set on the order of insobriety and sobriety; no one can tell what will be his state at the last!

The caravan which journeys under the shelter of God's grace will rest in pleasure, and set forth again in splendour.

Hafiz, take in hand a cup from the fountain of knowledge: so may you obliterate from the tablet of your heart every image of ignorance.

CXXXIII

Whosoever possesses a collected heart and an agreeable companion, good fortune is his friend, and prosperity his associate.

The court of Love is a great deal higher than Wisdom. He kisses that threshold who keeps his soul in his sleeve.

Rich man! do not look with contempt at the infirm and the poor, because the wayside beggar has the chief seat of honour.

Your small sweet mouth is, perhaps, the signet of Solomon, for the impression of the ring of its ruby lip keeps the world under its seal.

So long as you are on the surface of the earth, consider power as gain, because Time keeps many powerless beneath the earth.

The blessing of the needy is the remover of trouble from the soul and the body. Who gains profit from the harvest who is ashamed of the gleaner?

O zephyr! tell the secret of my love to that sovereign of beloveds who possesses one hundred Jamshids and Kaikhosrus as her slaves.

Since she possesses a ruby lip and musky hair, I am proud of my beloved, whose beauty possesses these.

If she say, "I do not want a poor lover like Hafiz," tell her that the wayside beggar possesses sovereignty.

CXXXIV

Who told you, my soul, not to ask about my state? Depart stranger, and demand no news of the friend?

Because you are merciful and compassionate to your slaves, blot out my iniquity, and demand not why I sinned.

Do you desire that the fire of love should burn brightly? seek its story from the candle, seek it not from the morning wind.

He had no knowledge of the world of devotees who said to you—"Ask not the devotee concerning it."

Ask not the dervish-clad recluse for money: inquire not of the beggar if he can tell you how to make gold.

We have never read the story of Alexander and Darius: ask of us no tale but that of love and loyalty.

In the book of the wisest physician no chapter on love can be discovered. O my heart, inure yourself to sorrow, and seek not for any cure.

O Hafiz! the hour of the rose is here: talk no more about knowledge! Understand the worth of time, and demand nothing about How and Wherefore.

CXXXV

Wine and delightful pleasure! what are they? Joys with no abiding! We flung ourselves into the ranks of the profligate: let be what may be!

Unloose the cords of your heart, and consider not the sky's secret; for the thought of no geometrician has ever untied that knot.

Be not amazed at the changes of Fortune, for its wheel has counted thousands and thousands of like changes.

Take the cup with reverence, for it has been formed from out the skulls of Jamshid, and Kai Kobad, and Bahram.

Who can tell of Kai and Kaus? whither they are departed? Who has wisdom enough to say whither the wind has carried the throne of Jamshid?

Now I can understand how, from desire for the lips of Shirin, the tulip bloomed from the tears of blood of Farhad.

Come, O come, for at this moment I seek ruin from wine. Who knows but in such ruin we may find a treasure.

Perchance the tulip foretold the unfaithfulness of Time; for ever since she was born and has loved she never lets the wine cup depart from her hand.

The breeze of the earth of Mosella and the waters of Rocknabad have never suffered me to enjoy the wandering and travelling.

From the troubles of love what has come to my soul has come: may the eye of fate never wound his soul!

Like Hafiz, never take the cup, save to the sound of the lute, for the gladness of the heart is bound to the silken thread of joy.

CXXXVI

Without the sun of your countenance the day has no light for me, and life to me is only an unending night!

At the hour of my farewell to you, far from your face, no light remained in my eye from its ceaseless weeping.

Your image vanished from my sight as I exclaimed—Alas! this wilderness, no portion of it now remains inhabited.

Your presence averted Fate from my head, now in your absence it is not far off.

The moment approaches in which the watcher may say, "That ruined, forsaken one, is about to depart."

What would it profit me now, if my beloved were to trouble herself henceforth in seeking to visit me, when scarcely a flame of life remains in my wretched body?

Absent from you, if my eye can no longer run with water, say—"Pour forth your heart's blood, if nothing else remains for you to shed?"

Patience should be my remedy in separation; yet how can I endure it, when the power no longer remains?

O Hafiz, with misery and weeping you have abandoned laughter; for to him who is clothed in Sorrow's raiment, what care can there be for feasting?

CXXXVII

Would that life's coins were assayed, so that the cloisterers might hold their peace.

What I advise is, that the friends should give up all work and kiss the curling locks of the beloved.

Happily the companions caress the cupbearer's ringlets, when the sky allows them enjoyment.

How brave are the children of Youth in bloodshed, who with the arrows of their eyes make constant prey!

Dancing to sweet song and the voice of the flute is pleasant, especially the dance in which the hand of the beloved is held.

Do not brag of the strength of your arm of chastity before the loved ones, because in their army a fortress is conquered by a single soldier.

When the crow is not ashamed of planting its foot on the rose, it befits nightingales to hold the skirt of the thorn.

In order that the people of vision may make the dust of your path the kohl for their eyes, for ages they have taken the highway of your path.

Hafiz, the sons of Time do not care for the poor—it is better that the poor keep aloof from them.

CXXXVIII

Yesterday morning I chanced to drink a cup or two, and from the lip of the cupbearer wine had fallen into my heart.

From the joy of intoxication I was longing to call back the beloved of my youth; but divorce had befallen.

I dreamed that I might kiss those divine eyes. I had lost strength and patience on account of her arched eyebrow.

Saki! give the cup frequently, because, in the journey on the path, where is the lover who has not fallen into hypocrisy.

interpreter of dreams! give good tidings, because last night the sun seemed to be my ally in the joy of the morning sleep.

At the hour when Hafiz was writing this troubled verse, the bird of his heart had fallen into the snare of love.

Printed in the United Kingdom
by Lightning Source UK Ltd.
118230UK00001B/348

9 780974 566795